What People Are Saying

Scientific research has well documented the healing impact of pets on people. Melisa Pearce's Equine Coaching Method has taken this a giant step further. Reading these stories helped me to finally understand what this equine gestalt work looks like in process. These magnificent creatures, with their enormous capacity for love, can create an atmosphere of safety, trust, and honesty with their clients in far less time than in traditional therapy. Each interaction between horse and client is efficient, with deep impact. Through unconditional love and acceptance, they lead, sometimes nudge, the client gently into the heart, the true place of profound healing and transformation. These rich stories attest to healing and/or breakthroughs in many different situations.

Melisa Pearce, her dedicated team, and these angels-disguised-as-horses are truly the gift of healing for the 21st century.

~ Susanne Doucet L.P.C.

Growing up in New York City did not give me any interactions with or understanding of horses. They were not part of my world, except in the western TV and movie dramas of those times. Reading these stories and poetry on the healing energy of horses and their great love for humans is an invitation into that world. Traveling into the hearts of these writers and their equine companions moved me deeply. The horses' ability to be always in the moment, and in the truth, created a safety net that enabled their human counterparts to go deeply into traumas and places that needed healing.

I recommend this book wholeheartedly. I loved it.

~ Jyoti Wind, author of *Unraveling Mysteries: An Anthology on Women and Aging* and *The Creative Arc: An Anthology on Writing*

Once again I am inspired by the power of the Equine Gestalt Coaching Model and by the wide-ranging ways students and graduates are bringing its light into their personal lives and into the lives of their clients. These stories describe the dynamic of two coaches working together: one human and the other equine. What a powerful team for transformation!

~ Peggy MacArthur, Owner, Birch Corner Associates and Coach, Touched by a Horse Certification Program

Standing at the center of a circle of horses facing me head-on beside their handlers, I first experienced the power of equine healing. Rescued from histories of abuse, these horses willingly offered their love to another being whose deep pain filled their energy field.

Melisa guided me around the circle, prompting me with a simple stem sentence to speak my truth to each horse. Each responded energetically in its own way, taking on the heat of my pain and releasing it, offering acceptance—they knew too well the hurts from humans—and reconnection to the core of my soul. Little did I know then that these exchanges were not only bringing health to a fractured spirit but opening a path to my participation in the liberating work described in this book.

I believe each of us has two tasks in life: discover our purpose for being here and then live it fully. The stories in this collection reveal a variety of ways the writers are discerning their answers and, in partnership with horses, offering their own lives as light workers for healing. As I am sure will be the case for you, I delight in the diversity of encounters described and the gifts each person and each horse brings to their respective callings.

~ Bob MacArthur, President, Birch Corner Associates
and Coach, Touched by a Horse Certification Program

From the perspective of a facilitator, these stories reveal the multitude of reasons that this Equine Gestalt Coaching Method is so successful. The manner in which these horses tap their vast reservoirs of acceptance and willingness through compassion to aid in helping the individual to heal themselves is nothing short of miraculous. Their hearts will touch yours, much as they have mine over the years.

~ Mark Guynn, Owner/trainer Guynn Training Center
LLC, NRHA, AQHA, NRCHA Judge

Touched by a Horse

Equine Coaching Stories

Touched by a Horse
Equine Coaching Stories

Edited and with a Foreword by

Melisa Pearce, Editor

Touched by a Horse, Inc.
Niwot, CO

Touched by a Horse Equine Coaching Stories
Edited by Melisa Pearce
Copyright © 2013 by Melisa Pearce

This publication is designed to provide accurate and authoritative information with regard to the subject matter covered. It is sold with the understanding that the author and publisher are not engaged in rendering legal or other professional advice. If legal advice or other expert assistance is required, the services of a competent professional person should be sought.

Touched by a Horse, Equine Coaching Stories

ISBN: 978-0-9760415-6-6
LCCN: 2013912839

Printed in the United States of America

Touched by a Horse, Inc.
P.O. Box 1106
Niwot, CO 80544
www.touchedbyahorse.com

Cover and Book Design by Nick Zelinger, www.nzgraphics.com
Illustrations by Diane Halenda, pdhalenda@gmail.com

Cover photo by Kimberly Beer, Kim Beer Photography,
www.kimbeerphotography.com

Cover photo of certified Equine Gestalt Coach Clemma Dawsen,
Horse Mind Quiet Mind, www.horsemindquietmind.com

Manuscript edited by Melanie Mulhall, Dragonheart,
www.DragonheartWritingandEditing.com

Contents

*I dedicate this book, my work, and my heart for all time
to my beautiful and courageous daughter, Molly.*

1988-2013

To learn more about Melisa's daughter Molly please visit:
MollyPearce-EakerFoundation.org

Foreword

Horses of all breeds have always been my teachers, confidants, and most trusted friends. As a child I knew them as beings who took me into my own world of creativity, adventure, and deep emotion. Like many, I grew up in a home that looked good to the outside world but was fraught with angst, fighting, and strife. Horses were my refuge.

Growing up in a family I could not help, I grew with great resolve and commitment to make a difference in people's lives wherever I could. I made some bad choices and some smart choices for myself, personally, but always found my heart salve through my equine soul mates. As an adult psychotherapist and gestaltist, I found that the love, guidance, and sound lessons my horses had taught me were also available to others who simply had yet to discover them.

I began to formalize introductions between my clients who were not horse savvy and my herd. Magic began to happen. This was several years before the Internet was born and available to provide introductions to others who had followed the collective consciousness in the move to human horse connection for healing.

Today I work as a gestalt coach. My coaching partners are my horses who work alongside me in reciprocity through the Equine Gestalt Coaching Method (ECGM) I developed over twenty-five years ago. This method involves the horse as a sentient being with vision, wisdom, and expression, and me as coach or guide to release the client's own awareness from within. As a gestaltist I trust the process to unfold beyond the foreground, which we are aware of, into the background, where the unfinished business of life resides.

As I maintain awareness of both my own somatic energy in my physical body and my equine partner's vibrational somatic energy, we work in concert to bring out the somatic at work in our client. Through nurturing and coaching, the client finds equilibrium again and their own truth, which leads them to a new congruence of mind, body, and soul.

In 2008, as America's economy was stumbling, I received several e-mails and calls from people who had benefitted from my work and were asking to apprentice with me to learn my unique method. At first I was uncertain, but after contemplation with my horses I knew this would ultimately benefit both my herd and horses everywhere because they would finally be seen worldwide as the true healers they are here to be. Commonly only seen as animals of service to plow fields, pull wagons, compete for wagers, or carry us to the hills, they are so much more—and they offer to us so much more.

The stories in this anthology are those of some of our graduates and students who are just beginning their journeys of discovery. Deep in my heart and consciousness, and after twenty-seven years of working with them in this way, I am still touched by the horse.

Thank you for sharing a part of this journey with us.

Melisa Pearce
Lil Bit North Ranch
Niwot, Colorado
July 2013

Acknowledgments

In the writing and the compilation of this book there were many hands and hearts. My personal loss of my daughter, Molly, fell right as we were pulling it all together, and as would be expected, I fell apart. Many people picked up the pieces of this project for me and my gratitude bubbles over to you all.

To start, I would like to thank assistant editor and Certified Equine Gestalt Coach Annette Price for listening to me at Summit 2012 and encouraging me to take this project on this year and not wait another one. Annette, you did a fantastic job coordinating this project with your usual style and fun, pulling together its many facets. My hat is off to you!

A huge debt of gratitude goes out to our judges (Jyoti Wind, Susanne Doucet, Jan Guynn, and Annette Price) who, along with me, read all of the submitted stories in unedited form and assisted us in making the tough decisions on which ones were to be included in this first volume. It was not an easy task sorting through them and bringing individual thought to the selections. We appreciate the generosity of your time and professional insight.

Our contributing authors and poets, I thank you. You have been wonderful students. And in your expression of our EGC Method, your EGC experiences are truly touching. I am certain anyone who engages with this book will want to experience horses in this unique way, and our mission as light workers will be enhanced by your expressions here.

Blessed am I to have the staff and affiliates who supported this project. Leeanne and Risa, thank you for having kept our business and offices straightened out during the minutia a project like this adds to the mix. Kim Beer, thank you for your frequent availability at a moment's notice to gather necessary details needed for the production of this book.

Many artists are involved in this book. I send a special thank you to Nick Zelinger for pulling our separate elements together and creating both the cover and interior design. Each time I work with you I marvel at the results. Diane Halenda, your illustrations add so much fun and personality to each of our stories. Thank you. I am so blessed on many levels to have you in my world. And again, Kim Beer, thank you for bringing your many talents to this project. Your cover photo stole my heart from the get go. It truly speaks to the soul, offering visual proof of horse soul touching human soul on so many levels.

As with everything I write, my dear editor and friend Melanie Mulhall, you are a true gem. Every step of the way, especially after my personal loss of my daughter, which fell in the middle of our time line, I knew and felt you at my back moving this along. Words cannot express how much you have helped me when I truly needed you, professionally, and even more personally.

Thank you to all the horses in this book and all those horses, everywhere, we work with. You are light workers bringing forth your true calling as healers of the human heart. You amaze us every day.

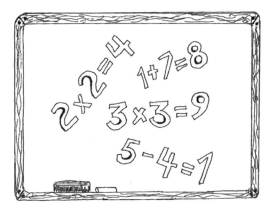

Romeo Love

Adrian Sparrow

"One times one is one. Two times two is four. Three times three is six—no, I mean nine. Eight times eight fell on the floor, pick it up with sixty-four." I hadn't done multiplication tables in years. What I had once memorized in fourth grade was giving my thirty-three-year-old brain a serious cramp. Despite my oncoming headache, I made my best left brain effort to keep running math problems through my head.

"That's good, Adrian," said Melisa Pearce, standing just outside the arena. "Stay in your head. Keep counting. Romeo wants nothing to do with you."

Romeo is one of the largest horses (okay, probably *the* largest horse) I have ever seen. I haven't been around a lot of horses in my life, but still, I know a big horse when I see one.

The curve of his back is taller than my five-foot-six head, and I have to stand on my tiptoes to put a halter on him, even when he so graciously lowers his head for me to do it. Horse people would tell you he's 16.2 hands, roughly 1,400 pounds. I'll just tell you he's a big boy.

I was alone with Romeo inside Melisa's large indoor arena at her ranch north of Boulder, Colorado. Romeo was loose in the arena, wearing no halter or tack of any sort. Au naturel. It was just me and a very large, loose horse that I didn't know very well.

Suddenly, standing there by myself in a big arena—alone, exposed, and with nowhere to hide—I tapped into what it must have felt like to be a gladiator. All eyes in the place were on me, waiting to see what this animal would do to me. I was the show, or so I thought.

Although I had no idea what to expect from Romeo and therefore no expectations about how this whole experiment should turn out, I could feel the anxiety mounting in my body. Something was stirring somewhere deep inside my cells. My brain was trying to tell me I was in an arena with a starving, pissed off tiger, while my body was picking up on something much more subtle. My energetic body already knew what was about to come with Romeo—and it was preparing.

I knew my life wasn't in any danger, really. Plus, Romeo wanted nothing to do with me. He was clear on the other side of the arena, minding his own horsey business sniffing the ground, looking for food, stra-la-la-la-ing—whatever it is horses do. He seemed as content as could be, as if he were outside on a sunny day, nibbling juicy grass in the pasture. And I was in my own world on the opposite side of the arena, doing math. We were as far from each other as we could possibly be—physically, energetically, and emotionally.

Pleased with Romeo's distance and disregard for me, I made a quick assessment. *I'm in my world, he's in his. This is familiar. This feels right.* Okay, then. With my head down, eyes focused on the arena floor dirt, and hands in my pockets, I began walking around in big, haphazard circles. Still counting to myself, I followed Melisa's cues and focused on "thinking."

Thinking is what we humans do naturally, all the time. We live in our heads, jumping from thought to thought like a monkey jumping from tree to tree. "Monkey mind" as meditation gurus call it. Whether we're rehashing what we should have said in that business meeting yesterday or planning our next trip to the grocery store, we keep our minds on the treadmill pretty much nonstop.

From her perch outside the arena, Melisa coached me to stay in that monkey treadmill state for about three minutes, maybe longer. I had no awareness of time passing. In fact, what I noticed during that time was that I didn't notice much at all. I don't recall paying attention to where I was walking. I don't recall being aware of where Melisa and the other student coaches were outside the arena. I don't recall if I felt warm or cold or if the barn door was open. And I almost entirely forgot Romeo was even there. I was so darn caught up in getting an "A" on my self-inflicted multiplication test, I became completely unaware of my surroundings. I was oblivious to any physical sensation. I zoned out my environment and shifted into autopilot like the time I pulled into my driveway, shifted into park, and realized I didn't remember getting there. The route was so familiar, I checked out, let my mind wander to who knows where, and unconsciously drove myself home. Scary. It's even scarier to think how many other unconscious drivers were out there sharing the road with me.

"Now, Adrian," said Melisa softly, pulling me back to the moment, "I want you to stand still and stop doing math in your head."

I stopped counting, turned to face Melisa, and closed my eyes, faintly aware that Romeo was still on the other side of the area, his rear end facing me, nose in the ground, clearly not stalking me. I don't think he even knew I was there.

"Feel your boots in the dirt, your feet on the earth," said Melisa. "Take a deep breath."

I happily relinquished the mind war I had been engaged in and settled into myself. I felt the heaviness of gravity securing my feet to the soft arena floor. I felt the mass of my body again and became aware of my face, my hands, my breathing. My whole body relaxed. It felt good, peaceful, like when I cuddle with my kids and sing them to sleep. I took a deep breath and smelled the pungent, earthy sweetness of dirt and animal. I heard hooves on the ground from the other horses in the barn. I heard hay being shuffled in their stalls.

"Now, Adrian, find your heart," Melisa said, encouraging me on.

I turned my awareness to my chest area and breathed in fully.

"Find that place in your heart where there is pain."

On my exhale, like water from a hose that had been kinked for too long, my tears burst to the surface. This was what my body, only a few minutes earlier, knew was about to come.

"Yes," said Melisa, quietly, "that's it. Let the tears come. Romeo sees you now."

The tears caught me off guard. I didn't know exactly what my pain was about or what the source of it was, but there was pain. The sadness didn't need a name, or reason, or explanation, it just needed permission to be felt. Through tear-blurred eyes, I glanced in Romeo's direction. He was walking straight toward me.

Holy shit. He sees me. He feels my pain from across the arena. He is coming to comfort me.

My heart ached, literally. I could feel the heaviness in my chest. The tears came even quicker, leaving salty paths on my cheeks as they carried years of sadness and pain up and out of my body and onto the dirt floor.

I've been discovered. Crap. No more hiding. He's coming. I desperately want him to, but I'm not sure I can handle the intensity of him being near me. I'm about to lose something I've held on to for so long. Don't take it from me, Romeo. It's all I've ever known.

And then Romeo was behind me. My eyes were closed, but I could feel his warm breath on my back, greeting me, acknowledging me, ever so softly brushing the back of my heart.

This horse cares about me. I'm hurting inside, and he cares. He doesn't care why I'm crying. He doesn't demand I stop because it makes him uncomfortable. He doesn't get defensive. He doesn't slam the door and call me a crybaby. He just wants to be with me in my pain.

Without saying another word, Melisa let Romeo work his magic. Quietly, we all stood in that arena, observing one of

God's greatest creatures do what he does best: give love. And I was the chosen recipient. Romeo instinctively moved toward the front of my body so he could have better access to my heart. He lovingly placed his soft nose near my chest and stayed there for several minutes.

My heart beat faster. My stomach began to hurt with more pain that needed to be released. Romeo was pulling a long chain of pain out of my body. And all he was doing, from what I could see, was standing near me.

Why do you care, Romeo? You don't even know me. Who am I to be worthy of your attention?

I saw visions of those who had hurt me, times I'd been betrayed, lied to, ignored. I saw myself hunched over in agony, crying and screaming in rage. He knew the truth. My truth. He saw through my "have it all together" façade. Yeah, this girl has some pain. She's been hurt. Her heart has been broken. It's not safe for her to love. Love always ends up in hurt and betrayal. She doesn't trust love. Her heart is like a bank vault, welded shut in protection and self-preservation.

Romeo stood there at my heart, still, energetically moving the long stored emotion out of my cells and out of my body. I was exposed but safe. Vulnerable but in loving care.

With my ego silenced and my heart gaping open, my mind went blank. It was just me, my tears, and Romeo.

I didn't know where Adrian ended and Romeo began. As Romeo surveyed the imbalances in my emotional body, our energy fields became entwined like a double helix. He filled in the places where there were holes and removed excess where it was no longer needed.

As the sea crawls onto sandy shore and erases all that was, so, too, did Romeo leave a wave-washed, untouched surface, born anew, ready to tell a new story with fresh footprints.

My tears slowed. I sniffled and wiped my wet face with the back of my hand. With a weepy smile, I touched the side of his face and stroked his long, broad neck. I weaved my fingers through his black mane, making little twisty braids. Touching him brought me back to Melisa's ranch, back to the arena, back to my body and place in time.

I made eye contact with the other student coaches who had been witness to the interaction between Romeo and me. Each one of them looked back at me with compassionate eyes and soft faces. I noticed the other horses in the barn at their stall doors. They had observed their colleague's work with curiosity. I felt seen; I felt loved—not only by Romeo, but by every soul in that barn.

My chest expanded and I felt warmth blossom from my heart chakra in all directions.

With perfect timing, Melisa intercepted the moment. "Beautiful," she said, smiling, as if knowing all along how this was going to turn out. "How was that for you?"

"It was amazing, and powerful," I said, "and surprising."

"I don't know specifically what I was crying about. All I know is that I wanted to cry even more when I saw him coming toward me. I'm used to my husband running away from my tears." I struggled to get the last sentence out as I spoke through more tears. "To have him come toward my pain was the most genuine act of love I've ever experienced."

"Did you see how fast Romeo tuned in to you when you got out of your head and into your heart?" Melisa asked. "It was instantaneous. You accessed your pain quickly, and he felt that big-time."

I felt it big-time, too. In my head, Romeo wanted nothing to do with me. In my heart, in my truth, Romeo wanted everything to do with me. And that was a foreign feeling for me. To have someone see right through me, to my core—to my soul—and not react with fear, judgment, or agenda, but to actually *love* me for what they see was something new. I didn't know that kind of love existed. That was for princesses in fairy tales, not me.

Yes, me. He simply was there for me. For Adrian. He didn't care how long it took. He didn't care if snot was dripping from my nose from all the crying. He didn't care if my mascara was smeared down my cheeks. He didn't care who was watching. And he didn't care how preoccupied I had been only a few minutes before, mindlessly wandering around the arena doing math problems, ignoring his presence.

This is just what he does. When he senses a human in pain, he comes running. This was Romeo love.

Prior to being seen (which I now equate to being loved) by Romeo, I didn't know what real love felt like. I had been closed off for so long, not wanting to let love in for fear of being hurt again. But even bigger than that, I didn't love myself enough to let myself *be* loved. Deep down, I didn't feel worthy of it. So I successfully repelled any love that tried to come creeping around. Shield up, armor on, ready for battle. Bring it on, wild animals and all.

But Romeo wasn't in it for the glory of the fight. It wasn't about cheap, thrilling entertainment for craving spectators.

Part of me did die out there on that arena floor, but in that dying, a purified version of me was released. And I knew this version of me could learn to love—and really live—for the first time in my adult life.

It was early April. I would be turning thirty-four in a few weeks. My relationship with my husband was struggling, but somewhere deep in my heart I felt hope. I could see into the future like never before. I was worthy of love. I was worth it. I was worth fighting for.

You killed me with your love, boy. The peace I feel in this moment was so worth the pain.

After letting me love on him for a few moments, he lowered his head, stretched his neck out long, opened his mouth, and began leeching. It's what healer horses do when they have absorbed a human's energy and need to release it out of their own bodies. If you were to yawn and gag at the same time, that's what it looks like. Romeo yawn-gagged a few times, then walked off, as if to say, "My work here is complete."

Just another day in the office for you, eh Romeo extraordinaire?

Melisa debriefed the other student coaches in the arena about what they had just witnessed.

"This," she said, with her arms outstretched toward Romeo and I, "is a perfect example of how horses experience humans."

She went on to explain how humans are agenda-oriented and ego-driven. Most of us live in an emotional state that horses can't—and won't—relate to, as showcased by me, when I was walking around the arena solving math problems. As soon as people check out of Head Hotel and check into Heart Hotel, horses are interested. Romeo tuned into me as soon as I took a deep breath and dropped into my body. His "sentient being" radar went off and he came straight at me, like a laser. In our heads, we're working from past experiences, unconscious programming, fear, limits, and lies. In our hearts, we're working from the here and now, love, potential, and truth. That's the language of equus.

I thanked Romeo, telepathically, for the love and healing he had so freely given me. I directed my heart chakra toward him and let a warm glow of light shine his way. In a period of less than fifteen minutes, my heart was opened. After lying dormant under a long winter's snow, Romeo brought my heart back to life. I could feel green, lush vines encircling my heart, hugging it back to life.

Romeo, Romeo, where for art thou? I'll tell you where he is.

This bay American Quarter Horse gelding, born March 17, 1999, lives at Lil Bit North Ranch with a herd of equally amazing heroes and heroines.

Oh, Romeo, you with world champion bloodlines and a successful show career in your past, you will forever be my champion, my fairy-tale hero. I don't care how many prestigious titles and belt buckles you have won in your day. You did your finest work today here, for me, in this arena.

Clearly, this is what you were born to do.

Romeo love. God's love. Amen!

Adrian Sparrow, a forever student and explorer, found her way to horses in 2011. With a desire to reconnect with nature and her own soul, she enrolled in the TBAH Equine Gestalt Certification program. She knew the program would be a stretch—having no prior horse or coaching experience—but she also knew the horses were calling. What she didn't know is that they would open her heart to an entirely new way of being in the world. Adrian lives a blessed life in Superior, Colorado, with her husband, Barry, and two magical souls who decided to be her children in this life.

Adrian Sparrow
Peaceful By Nature, Inc.
www.peacefulbynature.co
adrian@peacefulbynature.co

Begin Again ... with Horses!

Terri Mongait

Awareness—something we all take for granted. But on this particular day it was very important to me. I became aware that I was lying in bed. Recognition set in as I saw three friends I used to work with.

"Hi. What are you guys doing here? And where are we?"

Scanning the room I noticed I was in a single bed and behind a glass partition. There was a lot of activity beyond the partition, but it did not yet register. I turned to the other side of the room and saw my brother, Chris. Chris lives in Massachusetts, clear across the country from me. Now I was very confused. It did not make any sense.

"What are *you* doing here? And where *are* we?"

Then I realized that I had a tube in my nose and wires in my arm and elsewhere. What the heck was going on? Finally seeing my wonderful husband, Peter, I knew I was safe, but that still did not explain things.

I was told (not for the first time apparently) that there had been an accident, a riding accident. I was in the ICU and had been there for three weeks. That couldn't be right. Three weeks of my life gone? No, it must be a mistake. Surely I was fine. I wanted the tubes and wires off me and I wanted them to let me go home. I wanted to see my dog. I asked Peter to take me home.

Unfortunately, that was not allowed. While it did not register immediately, I learned that I had not only been in the ICU for three weeks, I had been in and out of consciousness. My sister, Claudia, had been there with me and Peter for the first difficult week of medical decisions. She was able to help Peter understand the medical jargon because she is an RN, and she had made sure I was well cared for. For a period of time they packed me in ice to keep my temperature down and she had also kept me dry. And she had made sure the nursing staff knew I was a vegetarian.

One side of my head had been shaved and a shunt put in my skull to monitor intracranial pressure (ICP). If the ICP exceeded a certain number they would have to operate to relieve the pressure buildup. I am grateful to Spirit that I did not have to have surgery. The technical medical term for my diagnosis was traumatic brain injury. It will always be a part of my life. After more days of recovering my awareness, I learned what had happened.

It had been a beautiful fall day—not too hot, a beautiful sun shining, the scent of dry brush and sage wafting on the breeze. Bodhi (my eighteen-year-old Quarter Horse gelding) and I were trotting up the trail.

Bodhi had been a part of our family for about four months. Prior to us, he'd had a difficult life. He had nerve damage to his neck and the side of his face thanks to a very bad accident in which he had gotten his head caught between the stall door and the wall. Someone found him in the morning hanging in the doorway. His lip hung down on one side. When he became part of our family, I did massage and energy work on him. His lip was almost all better.

I had been working with Bodhi, helping him to establish trust in me and relax on our trail outings. He had the difficult and annoying habit of backing up whenever I asked him to stop—not terrible if we were in an arena or round pen, but dangerous if we were on a riding trail with any kind of drop-off. Apparently, this had not been a good end of our ride. One minute I'd had Bodhi in an emergency stop, the next I had been in the air on my way to a very hard landing on my head. Paramedics had been called and after they determined I had sustained a possible brain injury, I had been airlifted to the University of Southern California Medical Center's intensive care unit.

I received an outpouring of love and healing energy from family and friends. In the months before my accident, I was enrolled in Melisa Pearce's Equine Gestalt Coaching Method (EGCM) program. I was a member of the first class and many of my herd mates (fellow students) were well versed in energy healing methodologies. Melisa was in touch with Peter and was monitoring my situation. Together with the EGCM herd, they surrounded me with positive healing energy.

I truly believe I am still here because of the energetic healing I received from my herd mates and because I have healing work, partnered with horses, to do. Both of my horses have played a huge role in my healing. After two months of hospital and rehab it was another few weeks before I could go to the barn and see my horses. It was because of my relationship with them that I forced myself up to the barn every morning to care for them and, most importantly, to learn about how my new brain wiring would work, explore my deeper understanding of their communications, and receive their healing energy. Not only were they helping me heal physically, they were helping me heal emotionally and energetically.

I could have said to myself, "Poor me. Why did this happen?" Instead, I choose to look at the accident as a necessary experience and an opportunity to rewire the neuro-pathways in my brain so I can accept that I do vibrate at a higher frequency than others. How fabulous that I can understand horses (and all animals, but mostly horses and dogs) on a deeper level and can share their spirit, wisdom, and healing with people. My head injury was a necessary step in my life's journey of helping horses heal humans.

Now that I am aware that I process things differently than I used to, every time I'm working with my horses, I stop and wonder when they react to something. "Hmm. That's different. What is this about?" I check myself and determine if they are telling me something about me that I might not be aware of or if something else is going on that I need to focus on.

Horses live life in the present moment—an important life lesson that I have come to embrace. This is also tremendously helpful when we are working with clients. The gift of my brain injury is the new ability to be curious and see the joy in everyday occurrences. Because I am able to work with horses on a daily basis, I find that I smile a whole lot more and have confidence in myself. I believe my equine coaching business is where my passion and joy lie. I get to assist horses in their healing of humans. Everyone benefits.

A major part of my healing has been through my work with horses. I'm back riding and working with clients. My own two are still working on healing with me. This has only served to reinforce my belief that at this time in the vibrational planetary shift, equus is here to help humans heal and evolve.

By planetary shift, I mean the energy changes happening all around us at this time in our realm. Many are already aware of the abrupt end of the Mayan calendar on December 21, 2012. Some have predicted the end of humankind as we know it, as well as cataclysmic planetary changes. What I believe is that Source energy (or God, Goddess, Spirit, whatever you call it) is telling humans that it is time for us to adjust our vibrational energy and evolve. Not necessarily leave the planet, but kick up our vibrational frequency a notch. The signs are all around us if we stop, look, and pay attention. We must evolve as a species if we are to continue to survive.

It makes me smile and warms my heart chakra to realize that equus is here to support and help us on this journey. Horses have been a part of man's journey for centuries and they willingly offer us a helping hoof. They have been with us when we rode them to hunt for food or went to war with other tribes. They were with us as we crossed this great nation, pulling our wagons and carrying our supplies. They stayed with us as we plowed fields and grew crops. They helped us build cities and plant roots. Their relationship with us has changed over time and they are now often here to give us pleasure, joining us in the show ring and rodeos. Yet they are still willing to help us on our own journey. They teach us patience and show us how to live in the present moment. They teach us to look at things from a different perspective.

Many humans are experiencing within themselves the breakup of old ego-based mind patterns and the emergence of a new dimension of consciousness. There is a large scale opening of spirituality. The ground for a more profound shift in planetary consciousness is being laid. This shift is destined to take place in the human species. This is the spiritual awakening we are beginning to witness now, and the horses are here to help us navigate this shift. As you work with a horse, a shift takes place within you.

Each day with my horses I am blessed with healing energy. To care for them I have had to increase my stamina, strength, and humor. When I run into a processing error I smile at myself, take a deep breath, and figure out how to keep both me and my horse safe. They are very patient, and yet I know they test my boundaries and help me to expand.

It took me about a week after being home from the rehab hospital before I felt strong enough, physically and emotionally, to go up to the barn and see my horses. It had been two months since they had seen me. I'm sure they knew what was going on because they hear things they understand and communicate with each other.

My husband drove me up to the barn the day after Thanksgiving. He helped me out of the car and we went to see Smarty first. As alpha mare, she expected me to see her first.

She was still eating, but in between grabs of hay, she came over to the stall door where I was standing. She seemed both unconcerned and happy to see me. She placed her forehead down for me to scratch and sniffed me from my shaved head to my heart chakra. When she shuffled and looked me in the eye, I heard in my mind, "Nice to have you back. It's about time." Then she went back to eating.

Now it was time to see Bodhi. Since he was the one I came off of, he did know a lot of what happened. As we walked up to his stall, I noticed he was standing in the back with his head in the corner. I stood at the door, took a breath, opened the door, and stepped in. He turned his head and looked, sadly, over his shoulder at me. When he saw it was me he nickered, then turned and walked toward me slowly, with his head hanging down. I kept hearing, "I'm sorry. I didn't mean to hurt you. I'm sorry."

He stood in front of me with his head still hanging and I stepped up to him, put my arms around his neck, and said, "Dude, it's okay. I'm okay and it was not your fault."

He looked me in the eye and I tried to convey that I was being honest with him. I did not, and still do not, blame him. He let out a big horsey sigh and leaned into me.

I had to reestablish my trust and relationship with both horses in different ways. It took almost a full year before Bodhi and I learned to trust each other again. He no longer feels that he was either a bad horse or a dangerous horse. We both know, acknowledge, and honor the realization that he has played an integral part in my life's journey. If not for coming off him and landing on my head, I would not have had the opportunity to rewire the neuro-pathways in my brain. I would not have spent three weeks in and out of consciousness exploring my spirituality. I would not have opened up to the realization that the horses and I can help other trauma survivors navigate their way back onto their life's journey. It was because of my accident that I was able to identify my EGCM client niche: traumatic brain injury survivors and their caregivers. I have expanded that niche to include all trauma survivors.

The first time I saddled Smarty after the accident, I swear she had grown three inches and my saddle had definitely gained weight. Not to mention the fact that as soon as I got the saddle on her, she started moving around. Saddling and cinching a moving target certainly increased my hand-eye coordination, whether I liked it or not. Apparently, she had lessons to teach me and healing to help me with. Together we took every step on our journey—mine toward improved health, strength, patience, and understanding and hers toward trusting that I would be with her every day. Together we are now well and happy. My new mantra whenever I hit a speed bump in my path is: *Pause, close your eyes, take a deep breath, smile and . . . begin again!*

I truly believe that if we humans would just be quiet and listen, equus has so much to share with us, as well as help us humans heal and evolve. My own healing is ongoing with almost all the horses I come in contact with. Every day I have to remind myself to get out of my own way, be open to whatever happens, and smile as Spirit comes through. I find the quieter I become, the more I actually feel and hear. It makes me smile when I think about all the changes I've been through since leaving the security of my corporate life. I want others to realize, embrace, and be okay with what I've come to call elective employment.

I am filled with gratitude every day that I go up to the barn and interact with my horses, even if it is mucking a stall or brushing a horse. When I left the corporate world and was struggling to reinvent myself, Spirit tapped me on the shoulder and held my hand as I took my first steps into the equine world.

Like many, midlife change of career women (planned or not) I was having a difficult time answering the question, "Who are you?" Most people answer that question with, "Oh, I am a vice president of marketing for (insert name of company)," or, " I'm a lawyer," or, "I'm an administrative assistant." But none of those are answers to the question. They express what you do, not who you are. I wanted to let go of what I did and fill myself up with learning who I am. And horses play a very important role in my continuing journey.

You never know when Spirit is going to offer up an opportunity. You just need to be open and receptive to issues and situations that, at first glance, seem random. For me, it was the opportunity to be blessed with the friendship of horses.

One morning I was out walking my dogs and a lady in a pickup truck stopped and asked me if I wanted company walking my dogs. I thought that a bit unusual, but I found out she was actually a neighbor, so I said sure. On one of our early walks she mentioned she had two horses boarded at a nearby facility. I said I had always wanted to learn to be comfortable around horses and she invited me to join her at the barn and help her walk her horses on the trails in the hills near our homes. Hiking, horses, nature . . . as far as I was concerned, it couldn't get any better than that.

But I was wrong. It did get better. I now own two horses of my own and have reinvented myself and my career. I am a wellness and life coach, and my horses are my co-facilitators. Working with the horses, I am honored to help people heal, better themselves, understand their past, reinvent themselves, overcome obstacles, and help grief to move on. This would not have happened if I had not been open to Spirit's message to me.

I believe that certain special things, people, or animals come into your life when you need them the most. Horses did not enter my life right after I left the corporate world. I had to gather the appropriate knowledge and life lessons before I would be ready and open to the healing gifts of equus. I became a certified massage therapist. Then I added energy balancing, Reiki, and craniosacral therapy to my expanding toolbox before I was presented with my equine gestalt coaching opportunity. I loved working on my clients, but I did not like working for someone else. That was what I did in the corporate world. I was also not comfortable with marketing myself.

So one day, not long after I acquired Smarty, I was massaging and doing some energy work on her when I felt as though we were being watched. I looked up from her stall and saw that almost every other horse in the barn aisle was watching what I was doing and I heard from them, "Ooh, can I be next?"

Yes, it was back to school for more education, and I became a certified equine body worker. Considering how much horses give to humans, I thought it was wonderful for me to be able to give them some healing in return.

It was not long after one of my wonderful canine companions Sierra passed away that I went to work on a favorite client, a handsome Paint gelding named Quinn. As I greeted him and walked over to begin my work, he walked away. I thought that was different, so I gave him a moment and then walked over to try again. Again, he walked away. I turned my back to him and examined my own energy to determine if he was feeding off something I was emanating. While my back was turned, he walked over, put his third eye chakra (center of his forehead) against my heart chakra (middle of my shoulder blades). And I heard, very distinctly, "You need healing more than I do today. I can wait until you are ready." He knew I was not over the loss of my Sierra, and he helped me heal.

Two years after my accident, we were blessed with the opportunity to pack up and move from Southern California to Sedalia, Colorado. Now my horses, mini burro, dogs, and chickens live on six acres in the foothills of the Rocky Mountains.

I have continued my EGC journey. That has included working with three therapists from Craig Hospital, the leading traumatic brain injury and spinal cord injury hospital in Colorado. I wanted to give the therapists the experience of dealing with a brain injury. I had one of the therapists in the middle, playing the role of the brain, and the other two on either side as the arms. The arms could only do what the brain told them and the brain could not use her arms. Then I blindfolded the therapists playing the arms so they could not anticipate what the brain would tell them. Their task was to untangle two halters and then halter the horse that was with them in the round pen. It went perfectly. The brain and arms got very frustrated. Smarty kept coming over to check them out and assess their progress. They never even got to the horse.

After I stopped the exercise we debriefed and I said to them, "From those few moments of frustration, you now know how your traumatic brain injury patients feel when they know what they want to accomplish but can't process the steps to complete the task."

The "aha" look on their faces was the icing on the cake. They were blown away and all hugged me and thanked me for the enlightenment. They also hugged Smarty for her patience and quiet participation.

A very important lesson I have learned from this journey is that everything I do with and for my companions (two-legged and four-legged) is a partnership based on love, trust, and support. I trust my horses will be there for me, and they trust that I will lead them and keep them safe. I trust that all my clients have the ability to heal and grow, and they trust that I will support them and help them navigate through their process, no matter how long it may take or how difficult it may be. We are on the journey together as trusting, sharing, and caring partners.

My work gives me the opportunity to help horses heal humans. With understanding and patience, my Touched by a Horse herd members helped me complete my studies and receive my Equine Gestalt Coach certification. My husband, horses, mini burro, dogs, and I have moved to our own equine facility—Begin Again Ranch—in Sedalia, Colorado. Partnering with my herd of wisdom horses, I help traumatic brain injury survivors and their families rebuild confidence and tackle new challenges. Together we coach people through life issues, trauma survival, self-esteem, relationships, empowerment, and grief and loss obstacles on their road to recovery.

Finding out about yourself with the aid of a 1200 pound sentient being is not something you forget. I am still on my own recovery process and I thank Spirit every day for leading me to Melisa's Equine Gestalt Coaching Method program as part of my life journey. My business tagline, "A Journey of Self Discovery through the Wisdom and Spirit of the Horse," sums it up completely. And since my recovery from my accident I have added, "Begin Again . . . with horses."

Terri Mongait was born in Queens, New York. After working many years in Manhattan as an executive/legal secretary she was offered the opportunity to move to Burbank, California, when her boss was offered the position of General Counsel for The Walt Disney Company. Terri spent thirteen years with Disney as a Senior Executive Administrative Assistant. In 2002, she left Disney to pursue a more healing career and became a certified massage therapist and energy worker. Along with her massage practice, she held the position of President for the California Chapter of the American Massage Therapy Association. After acquiring her first horse in 2007, she went back to school and received her certification in Equine Bodywork. She then pursued her current career as an Equine Gestalt Coach, moved her family and horses to Sedalia, Colorado, and now offers Equine Assisted Recovery at Begin Again Ranch.

Terri Mongait, EGCM
Begin Again Ranch
www.BeginAgainRanch.com
terri@beginagainranch.com

Message from the Equines

Glenn Weissel

Hooves Thunder,
Nostrils Flare,
Manes Sail,
Through Open Air

Galloping Beat,
Elders Speak,
We Hear,
"Let Go Fear"

Pain Revealed
Hearts Healed
Life Tastes Sweeter,
Love Reigns

Equine Mind,
Human Kind,
Souls Combined,
To Dream As One . . .

Of A Planet Healed

Influenced by his environment and inspired by living on Harmony's Heart Farm with his wife and family of horses, cats, and dogs, **Glenn Weissel** continues to evolve as an artist, photographing horses, people, and nature. Glenn is currently enrolled in the Touched by a Horse Equine Gestalt Coaching Method Certification Program. Glenn's niche will be to coach clients who are ready to dive deep into their own creative process. He is on track to graduate in 2013.

Glenn Weissel
VP and Chief Marketing Officer
Harmony's Heart Farm™
http://glennweisselphotography.com

Corporation Meets Equine

Carolyn P. Fitzpatrick

I was only five years old when I realized how much I was drawn to horses. As a little child, I made excuses to get out to the barn first thing in the morning, and I made excuses to stay until late in the evening. Everything about my pony seemed nearly mystical—his scent, how his muscles became more defined as he walked around the yard, the sight of him grazing. I was completely entranced. I was in awe of how his muscles and my hand fit just right in certain places, and I imagined myself riding bareback across big meadows with the wind whipping my face and lifting my mount's mane into the air. Sixty years later, I'm still entranced. To this very day, many of those same feelings surface when I am with my horses.

For the past four decades, I have lived on a farm in Virginia with ample room to support my horse passion. Many of those years, I have been an entrepreneur. In 2010 I learned of Melisa Pearce's certification program and became fascinated with the idea of learning ways to share the gift of the horse with others. Melisa's program was exactly what I needed to connect the dots between theory, credibility, marketing, and coaching—and do it all while being more involved with my horses as part of my business on a daily basis.

I quickly decided my equine coaching niche for my new business. It would include relationship building, life transition, women's empowerment, fear of riding, and grief from the loss of a pet. I felt I had more than sufficient background experiences from my own life and past areas of study for the first four categories. After all, I had been a mediator for more than twenty years and had listened to thousands of stories about poor relationships, lack of empowerment, and the uncertainty of transition. These were areas about which I had personal knowledge and could provide coaching questions that would open new insights for those searching for their own answers and direction. And after a near death experience from a horse accident, I had struggled with many emotions around riding versus not riding. Not riding was not an option for me because riding was like breathing. Riding without fear and with a feeling of oneness with my horse had always provided balance and my truest sense of self. But knowing this in my head was not the same as losing my fear after the accident.

I had also personally experienced how difficult overcoming grief was when a dear animal friend departed and I had no one close to me who understood my sense of extreme emptiness and loss.

Yep, I knew my niche.

I was shocked when I received an e-mail requesting a meeting to discuss a corporate retreat. I hadn't planned on giving corporate retreats. But if you just stay present with the work, sometimes the work you're meant to do finds you.

BB Harding and I had facilitated a spiritual journey workshop a little over a month earlier, and one of the attendees was the wife of the president of the corporate entity requesting this meeting. During the workshop, the president's wife had admitted that while she hadn't been convinced the experience would be meaningful for her, one of her friends had convinced her to attend in a moment of weakness. She had driven to the workshop expecting little gain from the day.

As it turned out, she gained a tremendous amount of insight and shared some of her experiences with her husband once she returned home. He could see that she was changed by the workshop and observed those changes for nearly a month before contacting me to see if I would put a fall retreat together for his executive team. I would never have dreamed our most skeptical participant at the spiritual journey workshop would have experienced such a personal impact that it transformed her into an advocate of the Equine Gestalt Coaching Method (EGCM).

Now, back to the day I received the e-mail request. My mind immediately returned to a discussion that I had some months earlier with my coach and friend, Bob MacArthur. I had told Bob that I had no interest in offering corporate retreats. I felt corporate retreats would be too impersonal. I also believed it would be very difficult for me to gauge whether the experience would provide the necessary environment for increased awareness and personal insights. I didn't have a lot of corporate experiences and just flat didn't have a passion for corporate coaching. Bob had very wisely stated that I should keep my mind open to all possibilities because as I moved through the certification program, I would identify endless possibilities of how to provide service in many arenas. At the exact time I read the e-mail from the president of the company requesting the meeting, I couldn't help but feel the irony of this situation. I was advertising for new business and the business coming my way was clearly in an arena I had planned to avoid.

After a few days and lots of contemplation, I mastered the nerve to respond to the e-mail saying that I would meet for further discussion about a possible fall retreat. I knew I needed to understand the president's expectations before I considered doing it, let alone invested the time planning it. I certainly couldn't promise or guarantee him any particular dynamic results or large company shift because the executive team had participated in a retreat.

Our meeting was scheduled for the following week. This gave me time to prepare a packet of materials and information that I could leave with the president, as well as make a list of questions we could address during the meeting. I wanted to understand more about the company and what they might want to get out of a retreat. I'd been an entrepreneur for a long time. I didn't consider myself the "corporate type" and I wasn't at all certain I would be a good fit for them. I knew that horses were great teachers and superb healers. I knew that the Equine Gestalt Coaching Method worked. But could a woman who planned to use the method to empower women and help people manage their grief over a lost pet actually be effective using the method with corporate managers? More to the point, would such a woman even want to use her EGC skills with corporate people?

The meeting was very productive and all of my questions were answered to my satisfaction. Whatever I might have thought of myself, the corporate president clearly thought I was the person to conduct the retreat. We agreed on terms and scheduled the retreat. Now my next step was to design what I would offer during the one-and-a-half-day retreat. As I left the meeting, I reflected on a couple of verses from the Bible: "Give to the one who asks you, and do not turn away from the one who wants to borrow from you" (Matthew 5:42); and, "'For I know the plans I have for you,' declares the Lord, 'plans to prosper you and not to harm you, plans to give you hope and a future'" (Jeremiah 29:11).

What the Lord's plans were for me were unclear, but the plan the president and I agreed to included meeting with the group at the company the day before they arrived at the farm for the retreat. When I arrived for that meeting, everyone was sitting around a large conference table—about as far from the barns, stalls, and pastures, which I was comfortable and intimate with, as you could get. I started with a brief bio of myself and then launched into the meat of the information that would prepare them for the retreat.

Before everyone left for the evening I reminded them of the time they were to arrive at the farm the next day and gave them instructions on what to wear and pack. Each participant made a commitment to be at the farm on time. They all left with smiles on their faces and seemed to really look forward to the following day's activities.

Before everyone arrived the next day, I gathered the tack and supplies I would need for the weekend. My professional handlers (Caroline Cohen, Liz Liverman, and Debbie Yakalavich) prepared the group circle in the indoor arena, making sure there were also chairs nearby for the handlers. The handlers also prepared the arena according to the plan I had developed.

The twelve participants began arriving about 8:15 a.m. for an 8:30 start time. As each participant passed through the barn aisle, I could hear them speaking to the five horses that flanked each side. I could only smile at that. Whether or not my horses were going to be the magical creatures for the participants that they were for me, I at least knew that they were workshop participant magnets—irresistible and enthralling.

I began with introductions, agreements, and some exercises I hoped would begin to open the participants to one another and the process. Next, I provided the horse safety demo. Then we got down to the "business" of accomplishing what they had come for. It would be fair to say that what we did was *anything* but business as usual.

It quickly became clear that the activities were providing useful information. Individual needs, group dynamics, the president's impact on his team—it was all being represented in both subtle and overt form in the exercises. And I relaxed into it a little because it was becoming obvious that people are people, whether corporate employees, entrepreneurs, stay-at-home moms, or any other way they could be grouped. They were still people with needs, fears, desires, and personalities. I could work with that.

Before breaking for lunch, we regrouped and did some processing. The participants were definitely getting into this new way of exploring how they worked as a team. They had no trouble discerning how things like communication, decision making, and confidence level impacted their ability to interact with one another and fulfill their own part in the process.

They had just never done it on a farm with horses before, and that difference allowed them to gain a bit of perspective.

Everyone then broke for lunch. It was quite comical to watch everyone grabbing their cell phones and checking their e-mails and voice messages before they gathered their box lunches.

The afternoon activities expanded upon what we had begun in the morning and gave them a chance to examine cooperation versus competition.

Their last outdoor experiment involved each member leading a horse through or over some obstacles. I used ground poles, cavaletti poles, cross-rails, pole ending poles, an "L," and an arch. I wanted this near the end of the day so each person could have a personal moment of pride in their accomplishments for the day. No one present was a horse owner. But in a single day's activities, each person had learned new things and could take pride in that. As I walked behind the group heading back to the indoor arena, I listened to their chatter and laughter. It had been a good day!

We ended the day with another round of processing and an activity designed to break down any remaining barriers between participants. We talked about observations, insights, and aha moments with some emphasis on bridging what we had done to how it might apply back at the office. I also gave them some time to say good-bye to the horses. It was clear to me that we had broken through to a level of authentic interaction because men and women alike were teary-eyed and hugging one another.

I thanked everyone for their honesty and good work and asked them if they had anything else they felt was needed before the day came to an end. The group had agreed to some terms for the day and one member wanted to form an agreement between the participants to continue with the terms when they returned to their company jobs. He also asked that a weekly meeting be held between them to keep each other abreast of their projects so they could support each other's departments in a better way. All were in agreement. The member who had made the special request agreed to type it up for everyone, make copies, and distribute it to them at work the following week.

Before they left, participants were given a chance to share some of their insights about the retreat. Among other things, it was clear that they had gained a new sense of just how unique each of their peers is. That was coupled with appreciation for that uniqueness. Each participant had a better understanding of their own style and how they could adapt it to work with others on the team. And they all saw the need for trust and respect—both giving it and receiving it.

For me, one of the best parts was that they all left exhibiting renewed enthusiasm for their team and what their team could contribute to the overall organization. I watched them leave thinking of superlatives like "awesome," "inspiring," "refreshing," "fun." I could hardly wait to design my next corporate retreat!

But did the retreat have lasting impact on the participants? You can never be sure, but I did hear from the CEO after the retreat. He admitted that he had been a bit apprehensive before coming. While his company had participated in numerous management training exercises over the years, including several Ropes Courses, they had never done team building or leadership training with horses. He said that he was amazed by how effective the program had been. His staff left with a better understanding of themselves and their fellow team members. They had forged a sense of how to better serve one another and the company and they better appreciated the differences between themselves and other members of the team. It was, he said, not only a unique experience, but one of the best seminars he personally had ever experienced.

Without a doubt, I am hooked on corporate retreats. They can require a lot more upfront work than some other kinds of retreats, but they can be as creative as you make them and the retreat can be so much fun for everyone. I feared that participants wouldn't learn as much about themselves during a corporate retreat as they would by participating in other workshops with a specific focus, such as relationship, transition, empowerment, fear, or grief. But every member left with a better understanding of themselves and their coworkers.

I had some new understandings of my own, thanks to that retreat. Whether a corporate retreat or a topic-centered workshop, each participant comes with their own anxieties, fears, and/or expectations. And since we are all human, our human emotions often drive the bus, whether in a family setting or a corporate setting. Interestingly, organizations are not unlike family structures. Participants in a company retreat have strong relationships with each other and there are some pretty classic dynamics between members. And just as understanding personal temperament and style is useful in family settings, it is useful to the members of a corporation.

The horses were definitely heroes at this retreat. Having them facilitate heightened the awareness of participants without making them feel judged by their peers. And the games I employed with the horses were a fun and novel way to give participants perspective, particularly when coupled with the coaching questions I used and group processing.

This retreat made a lasting impression on me because it made me understand that I had wrongly prejudged what a participant could gain from a corporate retreat. No, there were no deep personal breakthroughs as you might expect from other types of workshops, but there were huge breakthroughs of a different nature. During the day, I viewed a mature middle-aged man running from one activity to another with his camera in his hand to capture the moments of the day that he was sharing with coworkers. It was strikingly similar to a proud father filming his child seeing zoo animals for the first time.

I beheld the president exhibiting anxiety over the fact that his employees were witnessing his fear of entering a round pen with a horse. I beheld him again as he made good eye contact with his employees when he performed his task despite his fear, and then walked with a completely different stature as he led that horse to the next activity.

I witnessed a top executive express her greatest workplace fear and experience support, not criticism, from her coworkers after her disclosure. I watched a woman, who began the day afraid of the horse, end her day with smiles, laughter, and giggles of glee when she led the horse through and over obstacles in the outdoor arena. I heard a mother of three, who had been skeptical upon arrival, voice, as she left, that she had just experienced one of the most insightful days of her life. I listened as an introvert, who spoke little the first six hours of the retreat, found her voice and expressed that this was the first time she had ever really felt heard by coworkers.

Really, what more could I expect from a corporate retreat? And as a coach, what more could you hope to achieve with anyone? Without a doubt, I am hooked on corporate retreats.

Carolyn P. Fitzpatrick is a lifelong Virginia horsewoman who has years of personal experience with hundreds of horses of different breeds and backgrounds. For more than forty years she has combined her horse experience and her love for the "language of equus" with her extensive background in human psychology, conflict transformation, and relationship mediation. In the past four years she has developed her Trust-Based Equine Partnership training methods, which she teaches in a cooperative manner so the horse and horse owner learn to dance through life together with a stronger and deeper level of mutual understanding. Her desire to support other people led her to become a Certified Equine Gestalt Coach in 2012. She offers one-on-one coaching and workshops to assist others in understanding their past and to provide them with the tools to create a more fulfilling and rewarding life. She works from her training facility, Bellamy Farms, and also travels to other locations to make the training affordable for those who desire to host a clinic.

Carolyn P. Fitzpatrick
www.thehorseconnectionblog.com

Sweet Story

Lisa Aniballi

I have loved horses as long as I can remember. It all started on Coaltown Road when I was a toddler. I spent hours alone in the backyard, surrounded by pasture and horses. I played, napped, and basked in the horses' wonderful energy.

But growing up in the suburbs of Chicago, horses were mostly a dream, except the time when the Budweiser Clydesdales came down our street in a parade. To a girl who kept horse statues and read horse books, it was about the most exciting thing since I was given Barbie's horse, Thunderbolt.

I had a big boulder roped up with reins in our front yard. I spent hours there pretending I was riding a horse. I also pretended I was galloping through the wide open spaces while swinging high on the park swing and used rail fences as substitute horses whenever possible.

My cousin Sharon was also horse crazy and when we got really lucky, we were able to go to Kurtz Corral and ride ponies on the country roads in Door County, Wisconsin. Occasionally, while walking on the trails in the nearby forest preserve, we would meet horses and their riders on the trail. The riders often stopped and let us pet their horses. I thought they were the luckiest people in the world to have their very own horse, and still do.

When the family drove north to Wisconsin or west from the suburbs, we would play a game we called "horses." We would count the horses we saw first. White horses were worth ten points. A cemetery on your side of the road meant you had to start over. When the extended family got together in Fond du Lac, Wisconsin, the cousins got to ride the Beer Hut Horses. The Beer Hut was like an A&W with beer and a carousal. With every round of beer for our dads, we kids got to ride the horses.

When I graduated high school, I drove west until I found a barn—Horseman Stables. I went in and proudly announced I wanted to work with horses. The owner was only too happy to accommodate. He got free labor for teaching me the ropes. I had a job at the bank to pay rent and every other free moment was spent with the horses. I was learning to ride and jump, as well as how to care for the horses. While working there I fell in love with a beautiful chestnut Arabian gelding, Sultan. I wanted to buy Sultan and live happily ever after, but the owner of the stable had other plans. He didn't want to lose his free labor.

So things did not work out as I had hoped, but I did go on to live on a horse estate in Barrington Hills. There I took care of the estate owner's horses and worked at nearby barns, mostly in the hunter-jumper world. Some Sundays we rode in a hunt—champagne, hounds and all.

I eventually married, had a beautiful daughter, and divorced. But, all the while, horses were never far away. As soon as my daughter, Kristen, and I got our own place, we rode the neighbor's gentle mare around the neighborhood.

At thirty, I was a single parent without a career. I went to school to be an addiction counselor, and I was lucky enough to do an internship at the POWER Program, where I facilitated high and low ropes courses and adventure trips. For fifteen years I helped people to be comfortable in the wilderness so they could be open to the miracles that happen in the moment in the great outdoors. Then, I knew it was time to bring in animals and their wonderful healing energy starting with Murren, a beautiful Bernese Mountain Dog. We went through the training for therapy dogs. By this time I was working in a residential treatment center, and the boys who called Gray Wolf Ranch home would light up when Murren came bounding in the door. Horses were next.

It was just another day at Gray Wolf when Rob Meltzer, the educational consultant, came to visit the ranch. Before Rob arrived, I took a quick look at his website and not only saw horses on it, I saw that he did equine therapy. I also saw that he partnered with Melisa Pearce doing equine therapy.

We enjoyed a delightful day together. When Rob met Peter, the owner of Gray Wolf, he told him that equine therapy is the most effective, efficient means of therapy there is! Rob also invited me to come to the Naropa Wilderness Therapy conference in Boulder and Melisa's daylong workshop on equine therapy. That sounded great to me, although I was not sure my budget would support this undertaking. That problem was soon solved because the next morning, Peter asked if I would go to Naropa representing Gray Wolf. When Rob, Clemma Dawson (now a graduate of the EGC method), and I headed up to Melisa's Lil Bit North Ranch, near Boulder, Colorado, we were greeted by a veritable menagerie of animals—including two Bernese Mountain Dogs. I jumped right in and volunteered.

I even managed to do some work with Melisa and a beautiful young Paint mare named Something. I realized that the continual pain in the right side of my body was from a heavy metaphorical backpack I had been carrying, and between Melisa and Something, I left feeling much lighter and brighter. I extended my trip a few extra days and did an individual session with Melisa. I knew I wanted to become her student and learn the EGC method. Being the SJ that I am, I did my due diligence before signing up and entering the Momentum group. I was accepted on December 1, 2010, and started January 1, 2011.

There was no turning back!

I started spending more time at a local ranch to refresh my horse experience. One day when I was grooming the miniature horses, a beautiful Arab chestnut gelding caught my eye. He was new to the ranch and came from an abusive upbringing. He had been called Later because no one could get near him.

We instantly connected. After six weeks he was gaining weight and feeling better. It was time for him to move on to a forever home via craigslist. I wanted what was best for Later, but it broke my heart. I wanted to be his forever mom in the worst way.

I shared this with Ashara Morris, a fellow student in Melisa's program. She told me that every horse she felt that way about was in her herd, and she would take him into her herd if I worked with him for six months and it didn't work out. I agreed to this plan and the Arabian was mine. But with a new name: Sweetness, Sweet for short.

It was spring of 2011 when I fully realized why Sweet came to me. A well-known local healer and Five Element acupuncturist, Lois Barnett, came to experience EGC with Ben, a nine-year-old Tennessee Walker in my herd. Sweet was in the walkout next to the round pen to watch and learn from his mentor Ben. However, Sweet decided Lois was his to work with. He put his hoof up in a big way that day and did a lot of physical work with Lois.

Lois' well-being had been critically affected years earlier when she unknowingly stepped into the crossfire of some very negative shamanic warfare. An accident had also left her with significant nerve damage and loss of sensation in her hands, chest area, and heart chakra. For six years, every healer who attempted to help free her of this negative energy had been unsuccessful. Miraculously, Sweet knew exactly what needed to be done and did so before Lois even realized what was happening.

While Lois was drawn in by his youthful energy, warmth, and keen beauty, he began to pull things out of Lois that no longer served her. I asked her some key questions, like what was going on for her on the inside and outside. She focused within herself and then outside of herself on Sweet. His loving kindness and gentleness was remarkable.

This wonderful horse that I loved but was not sure would be ready to do the work had just been waiting for his opportunity!

"I was literally blown away by Sweet's natural inclination," said Lois. "And his ability to free me of this nasty energetic baggage when I least expected it, and simultaneously fill my heart with unconditional love and joy." Lois called me later that day to tell me she could feel her hands for the first time in six years. She was so grateful and in awe—and she quickly scheduled her next time with the horses. After the next session, she was finally able to feel her heart again.

Another time, Sweet brought out Lois' younger self to play. All the while, healing was happening on so many levels. When he was turned out after that session, Sweet reared up and ran off bucking, enjoying a good release. It brought Lois great joy to witness a physical release she was not presently capable of, but experienced through her horse friend Sweet. Sweet brought her authentic playful self back to life.

Sweet and Ben are quite a tag team too. Ben distracts Lois while Sweet literally pulls unwanted thoughts and energy from her.

As time goes on, the horses share more of themselves and their spectacular love and healing energy. All with a sense of humor too!

One of the ways we share this amazing work with those in the community is a weekly group. Every Saturday is unique and magical in its own way. During the time leading up to the group, I had been experiencing noticeable change as we passed December 12, 2012, and December 21 was quickly approaching. As the Mayan Calendar completed, we were heading out of one time period into a new one. Many believe that this new time period will be one of spiritual transformation. I was noticing changes and so were many others in my life. There were changes in the horses and the herd and changes in relationships. There were openings that did not appear to be there previously: more acceptance, invitations, and new, positive ways of being together. There were also changes of an opposite nature, such as the children and adults who lost their lives at Sandy Hook Elementary School.

The day after the Sandy Hook Elementary School shooting was gusty, possibly too windy to have group. But the horses know when it is time to work. They calmly settled in, ready for whatever would come up, holding space for the group. The group shared longer than usual, including a lot of talk and emotions about the events of the week. One of the group members brought her younger self in with Sweetness. She leaned against the stall wall and slid down to her heals. Squatting there, she was bathed in sunlight that streamed in through the stall door. At the same time, sideways driving rain was just outside the stall door. Sweet nuzzled her with great care. He worked his magic. It was a beautiful sight to behold. She returned to the group calm and relaxed and filled with love. Sweet then turned around to finish the group off with his grounding root energy.

Another group member spent time with Ben. Ben is tall, black, and handsome, and he loves to share his big heart and gentle nature with people. A seasoned group member went into the stall with Ben without expectations. She had a gentle visit and was beaming when she returned to the group.

In closing the group we have started a tradition of each person choosing an angel card and sharing its significance for them with the group. The cards chosen were surrender, forgiveness, simplicity, contentment, and a blank card to hold space for them all. The cards and the group were like the week, a real mixture of feelings and events, which felt totally appropriate. Somehow it was all okay, as it should be.

We stood silently in the cold, huddled with the horses, in quiet vigil for the families in Connecticut. Finally we realized why the baby Jesus was born in a manger. This is where the magic is—in humble surroundings, with the animals. This is the place to be. It doesn't get any better than this.

Every Saturday, Elizabeth (my horse handler), Ben, Sweet, and I plan for group. How many show up tends to vary. Sometimes it is Elizabeth, the boys, and I. One Saturday in January, Ben showed up as the physician. It was a chilly morning, and for the third week in a row, no one showed up. But Elizabeth and I proceeded. Elizabeth read a guided meditation that brought us to the polarity of masculinity and femininity.

We brought this to Ben in the round pen. With Ben and the polarity pole in place, Ben did a thorough exam of his "client" Elizabeth. He checked her out head to toe, not missing a thing, stopping in a few spots to clear unneeded tension, and to open up channels.

Elizabeth named each side of the pole, masculine and feminine, and then stood in in a neutral position near the pole. I asked her to describe her feminine traits and she was stumped. She asked me to tell her what they were. I encouraged her to try. Elizabeth's femininity was all tied up with caring for others. Mothering, nurturing, serving, and feeding, were all she could see in the moment. We talked about introjection and what she had learned from the women in her life while growing up. I asked her if this was connected with previous work she had done related to her former husband, and she said that it was. She made a decision to let it all go and sit in neutrality. When she did that, she came to a new place within, a place of freedom and beauty. Elizabeth beamed!

I said to her, "From today, as this thirty-five-year-old beautiful, confident woman who is clean and sober, confident, doing good things, and working with horses, how do you describe your femininity?"

Everything she said was beautiful. It was about being and not doing. Being who she is. Ben backed his root chakra into me. He kept firmly stepping backwards telling me, us, "She has everything she needs. She doesn't need to serve a guy or have a deal to be safe. It is all within her." At the same time, Ben's heart was right behind her. He was supporting her. Then he went to her and kept backing his rear (root chakra) into her directly, saying to her through his movement, "I support you, but you have what you need! You are safe and secure." He then turned around and backed into the fence while making faces of delight. The message being, "You can do it for yourself, and it feels good. You don't need anyone else. You don't need a man. All you need is within yourself."

Elizabeth felt confident, relaxed, and beautiful in her new sense of spaciousness. Light and easy; full of joy. I asked her if she could name the feeling and she said, "Angelic." She thanked Ben, the physician. He had examined her and prescribed the cure, with love, determination, and a sense of humor.

To close the group, we choose an angel card. Elizabeth's was "Obedience," with an angel on a motorcycle stopped at a stoplight. This beautiful angel had freedom and fun while being obedient to accepting and embodying the prescription to be true to herself and know she has everything she needs. My card was "Healer," which carried the image of one angel with healing hands on another angel. Ben the healer, me the healer, coach, and light worker for the horses. We were overwhelmed with the joy of what had happened that cool January afternoon in an old World War II era barn.

I got a phone call later that afternoon from Elizabeth who was on the ferry headed home to the other side of the water. She called to say that after years of therapy working on letting go of her ex-husband, he was gone. She was free and he was free! She was, and is, so grateful.

Me too. I am so blessed to do the work I love with people and animals I love. Life is so good. I have found my purpose and I have been guided to this place from day one. Thank you God, thank you God, thank you God!

Through all of this—life, groups, and the wonderful healing sessions—I have learned that everything is exactly as it is supposed to be, right on time and in the perfect place. It happens every Saturday. A little piece of heaven right here on the Olympic Peninsula in the state of Washington. Nicker, nicker.

Lisa Aniballi has worked in the field of addiction treatment for twenty years as a chemical dependency professional and outdoor specialist. Most of her work has been experiential: leading wilderness trips, hiking, backpacking, canoeing, kayaking, and horseback riding in the states and abroad. She has loved horses and dogs her entire life. When she learned of Melisa's program and was able to combine her skills of helping people in an experiential manner with the horses, it was exactly what she was looking for. Lisa graduated as an Equine Gestalt Coach in 2012. She has two beautiful healing horses, Sweet and Ben. She loves empowering people to let go of what no longer serves them and move into the life they desire. She provides individual sessions, groups, and retreats on the beautiful Olympic Peninsula, surrounded by the mountains, water and forest—a perfect combination of the natural world and equus to open, nurture, and restore souls.

Lisa Aniballi, B.A, C.D.P, Certified EGCM
Empowerment through Equus
lisa@empowermentthroughequus.com
www.empowermentthroughequus.com

Nothing Short of Brilliant

Annette Price

A dusty truck pulled into Grandpa's driveway and we all moved out to the front yard to see what was happening. The fellow who crawled out of the cab was wearing blue-and-white pinstriped overalls, the uniform of many Missouri farmers. When Grandpa was excited his eyes sparkled, and he certainly had that mischievous glint in his eye this day! His excitement was contagious and I found my excitement growing. All breath left my body.

The man led a red-and-white pony out of the trailer. He was the perfect size, the perfect color. He was brilliant in every way. My heart melted. I barely heard Grandma remind us that this pony was for all of us grandkids. My prayers had been answered.

My pony had arrived!

Fast-forward thirty-odd years. I had been fretting around my house all day, waiting. My sister and her husband were traveling from southern Missouri, bringing my new horse to me. We called this gorgeous registered Missouri Fox Trotter Lakota. I had been whispering to her for months, telling her about her new life in Colorado and how excited I was to share my life with her. My sister bought Lakota as a yearling, a gangly spotted bay with four white feet and a diamond on her forehead. I fell in love with her the first time I saw her on one of my trips back to my home state. Now as a green broke four-year-old, she was headed to Colorado.

My sister called to say they were close. I went out to throw open the gate so they could drive their big rig in and I hung on the fence, waiting. Lakota was glowing in the fading light as she stepped out of the trailer. She was bathed and clipped to show quality perfection, not a hair out of place after a whole day in the trailer. Eyes wide, nostrils flaring, and hearts pounding, we faced each other. I was ten years old again and every cell in my body was tingling. My sister placed her lead rope in my hand and said, "This horse will teach you patience."

We had no way of knowing what an understatement that would be.

Lakota and I were blessed to be living in an area where natural horsemanship was more than a spoken phrase and we had the opportunity to play and study with many trainers. As a youngster, she was not very confident and spooked at everything. She held me accountable and made me become a better horsewoman. We learned and grew together, doing ground work, arena work, and trail riding. We even played with cows, one of my favorite pastimes. Through the years we faced many challenges with varying degrees of success.

I continued to talk to her and told Lakota many things. One nasty January day, I looked at her and started crying. The wind had whipped her mane into a tangled mess, a series of gnarly dreadlocks that stormy fingers had woven into an ugly mat. It was hideous. I thought about going inside, getting the scissors, and just cutting it out. It was too much and it looked impossible. I had no tolerance.

I had just hung up the phone from talking with my mom. They had found more cancer in my dad. So there I stood in the cold sunshine beside my beautiful horse. I set down her comb and started at the bottom. With my fingers, I began to unwind the clumpy mess. Sobbing, sometimes barely able to see what I was doing, I felt my way through it. By the time I had finished, I had stopped crying. I was proud of myself for saving her gorgeous mane. I marveled at her patience, for standing there and being with me in my grief. In that moment, she was my sister, my witness, and my friend. And for that moment, I found peace.

For over twenty years I had been on a personal spiritual path seeking my own answers. I jokingly referred to my self-defined home study curriculum as "How to Be a Better Human 101." I found the study of energy to be compelling. I am not interested in how a lightbulb works, only that it does. But I *am* fascinated with the energetic connections of the natural world. I studied the physical and spiritual qualities of plants and animals and their relationship to us, which led to shamanic journey work and the study of classical Chinese medicine. I exposed myself to different ideologies to see what parts of them resonated with my own innate intelligence. I became a Reiki Master and studied other healing modalities, always amazed at how they complemented one another.

There have been several teachers who were instrumental to my development and many said, "You could work with horses if you wanted to." But when I asked what that meant, they only shrugged their shoulders, meaning it was yet another thing for me to figure out on my own. And try as I might, because I found the idea so totally appealing, I could not visualize it. I couldn't "see" it.

And then I found my next teacher. She was practically living in my backyard. How fortunate for us. It was a very serendipitous series of events that led me to Melisa Pearce, founder of Touched by a Horse. It was during the Christmas season of 2008, and she had begun putting together a course on Equine Gestalt Coaching Method. I found the idea fascinating but slightly out of my reach financially. Where there is a will there is a way and I found a way to make it happen.

I was six months into my studies with Melisa when I decided to take Lakota to class for the weekend. She excelled in every situation that Melisa placed her. Nothing short of brilliant!

Melisa placed my very willing mare in the sixty-foot round pen located inside her indoor arena. Melisa began working with a beautiful woman, my fellow student, helping her unwind a story that had been trapped inside her for a long time. It was emotional for everyone in the barn. Lakota stood watching and listening as if she understood every word. As part of the experience, Melisa had big helium balloons brought into the arena and instructed the woman to write messages on the surface using an ordinary Magic Marker. One of the balloons popped. It was as loud as a rifle shot in that large metal barn. We all jumped, and I immediately tuned into Lakota. She could have easily spooked, but she would have had nowhere to escape inside the pen. She has that spark inside her, a "very strong and well developed survival instinct" as a friend of mine once quipped, and not in praise. I would not have been surprised if she had reacted with panic at the loud noise. But she did not.

Lakota and I locked eyes and then we both looked at Melisa, who remained calm. I knew it was just a harmless balloon, but how could a horse know that? One of my horse trainers many years earlier had told me that horses aren't afraid of getting hurt, they are afraid of getting killed. That is the life of a prey animal, always on guard, always interpreting the energy around them. Their basic survival has always depended on their ability to read their environment.

The gestalt experience resumed and then another balloon exploded. I looked at Lakota, who was facing the two women, watching them intently and absorbing the shocking noise. Her body spasmed, but her feet never moved. I could only assume she overcame a strong instinct to bolt, resisting the fear. There was no doubt that she knew she was part of this woman's healing experience and she chose to stay on target. It was amazing to watch. The client was a horsewoman and fully understood what it had taken for the horse to stay present. Lakota was showing her how to be brave and face her fear. Nothing subtle about it. The message was silent but immensely powerful. Melisa ended this remarkable piece of work by taking us all outside to watch the balloons, once released, carry to the heavens the woman's messages, her prayers.

The next day Lakota once again joined us for a piece of work. This time a fellow student walked with Lakota in the round pen. As the woman walked and Melisa coached her through her emotions, my sweet horse stood in the middle of the round pen with her neck stretched out and her head hanging low. It started as a yawn, but it went on and on. She looked to me as if she were trying to throw up, which I knew was impossible for a horse. Was she choking on arena dust? Her eyes would close and she would pull her lips back to expose her teeth and gums. Her torso heaved. I was petrified. I wanted it to be over. I looked at Melisa and she did not seem at all upset with what was happening. It was all I could do to sit there and trust the process. What the heck was going on? As the session with the women came to an end, Melisa asked her how she was feeling.

With a happy grin on her face she replied, "I feel incredible, like I just lost a hundred pounds."

"I'm not surprised," Melisa said. "This dear horse has been leaching negative energy off you for the past ten minutes. You're definitely lighter."

Hands shot in the air. All of us wanted to know what we had just experienced. Melisa explained that horses have the ability to leach, or remove, negative energy from the human body. The horses do not hold on to that energy in their bodies. Instead, they allow it to pass through them. My previous Reiki training had shown me how energy can travel down our energy meridians into the earth. Mother Earth is not concerned with whether we think energy is positive or negative. Energy is energy, and she can use it to do all the marvelous things she does. But the important thing for me was that Lakota did not hold on to any "bad stuff" she had released from the woman, who was now beaming, having thoroughly enjoyed her session with my miracle healing horse.

My horse was proving to be a rock star of healing!

Lakota returned home when the weekend was over having already graduated as a qualified equine gestalt partner. I, on the other hand, had many more months to study, practice, and learn this fascinating skill set. But I stuck with it and graduated as a Certified Equine Gestalt Coach in June 2011. And Lakota was waiting, ready to go back to work.

The next summer I had a young couple come out to do a session with Lakota and me. They were referred by a mutual friend and were looking to "get out of town and have a fun time together doing something new." I introduced them to my friend Laurie, who was present to be my assistant, my horse handler, as we call it. They were not "horse people" but enjoyed the safety demo and some simple grooming exercises. At one point in the session, I consciously calmed myself down to enter what one of my teachers calls "the neutral zone." It is from this place of inner calmness that I can access the place from which I seek guidance. I basically prayed for guidance, for an exercise that would be the most beneficial for this lovely couple. I wanted something that they could do together, as a team, if possible.

Almost instantly, I had a vision of a blindfold obstacle course. Yikes! I had done several different types of obstacle courses in my EGCM training, and with Lakota, but never blindfolded and not with a young couple with very little horse experience. I was not at all comfortable with this idea. I found my neutral space again and calmly asked for "Plan B." Nothing, I got nothing. I was all alone in my little universe.

Well, it is more like having a foot in two different universes. Even as one part of me stayed present with two wonderful clients, I had a very quick dialogue with that part of me I call my "higher wisdom." This can be a tricky thing in any coaching situation, but when your business partner is a gorgeous but hefty one thousand pound horse, the stakes can be a little higher. But I do trust the gestalt process. And I have learned from years of cultivating access to this higher wisdom that I could trust my prayers would be answered. I had asked for help and received a reply. I just didn't appreciate the answer. And that, too, had happened before.

I left the couple relaxing in the shade and excused myself for a conference with Laurie. I told her what I had visualized, my ideas of what it would actually look like, and asked if she felt competent to help me execute this gestalt experiment. She agreed with raised eyebrows, which looked slightly skeptical to me. Her main job was to serve as another set of eyes for me, paying particular attention to the proximity of Lakota's feet to theirs, so that the two would never meet. I had several concerns, but I certainly did not want her to step on the blindfolded adventurer. I found a scarf to serve as our blindfold and went back outside.

I told the couple what we were going to do while Laurie put a halter on Lakota. They seemed excited about the prospect, and I was warming to the piece of work, myself. The afternoon had gotten really hot and I decided to run the course in my side yard to take advantage of the many large shade trees. As they decided who would wear the blindfold first, I casually positioned several chairs around the yard. When I returned, the wife was being fitted with the scarf and I congratulated her on being so brave. She laughed nervously.

She would take hold of Lakota's lead rope and her husband, following my silent commands, would talk her through the obstacle course. He could speak, but he could not touch his wife or the horse. We gave her a moment to reconnect with Lakota, which probably felt much different once her vision had been taken away. Using hand signals, I instructed the husband to ask his wife to move forward across the lawn. The three of them did very well together. He talked his wife around the chair, under tree limbs, and in and out of the cool shade. My horse handler remained silent but so observant. I was thrilled that it went so well.

When the moment felt right, I guided them back to where we had started. With very little talking, they exchanged places. I had watched the husband during the first phase of the experiment and had a very strong sense that he had memorized the course. Just to make sure, we made a game of spinning him around a few times before we handed him Lakota's lead rope. There was also no doubt in anybody's mind that he was securely blindfolded. His wife took good care of that. I now kept silent contact with her as she guided him out into the parking lot, between cars, around a hitching post, and back towards the shade of the yard. I was watching Lakota. She was acting differently, tossing her head about and bumping into the young man. I got Laurie's attention to protect his feet so I could concentrate on what I was observing. The woman was doing an excellent job of communicating with her husband and guiding him safely under a low hanging tree limb, and yes, Lakota was definitely making it difficult for him.

Was my horse intentionally misbehaving? I didn't believe that for a second. So it was my job to figure it out. What was Lakota doing or showing us?

When the threesome got clear of the tree, but were still standing in the shade, I asked them to stop. The gentleman reached up to his blindfold and I quickly asked him to please keep it on. I asked him what was going on for him. It was obvious from his answer that he was a little upset.

"Well, she's pushing me around and it's getting worse, not better."

"Is this indicative of anything that is happening in your day-to-day life?" I asked.

He was silent for a moment. He scratched his head and massaged the blindfold, but did leave it on.

"It reminds me of things that are going on at work. I own my own business. I have a partner who has gotten really pushy lately. He's a good friend of mine, but I'm not comfortable with the direction he's going in."

There was no way I could have seen that coming. I had no idea why Lakota chose to pantomime this scenario back to him. Or was it just an enormous coincidence? Ha!

I asked him to take a deep breath and get very calm. He understood the idea of "grounding" so I asked him to take a few more deep breaths, gather the energy of the earth beneath his feet, and bring that energy up into his third chakra, the center of will and determination. Laurie and I watched him take a wider stance and stand up tall. His shoulders moved back and down into a more relaxed position. His physical appearance changed from an anxious, hunched over protective stance to a strong and secure one. He looked tall and confident.

I sensed that he was finished with his personal grounding. I asked him to take another breath. Then I asked his wife to talk him around the rest of the course again. To watch them together was to witness the beauty of this work. Lakota was a perfect partner. She was totally respectful of his space and never once tried to move in on him. The husband looked comfortable and in command of the situation. He held the lead rope with a gentle authority. A complete transformation. Laurie and I once again locked eyes for a brief moment.

Are you seeing what I'm seeing?

Yes, I am! we screamed silently to each other.

The exercise ended shortly as the team of three worked themselves back to the place of beginning. He excitedly pulled off his blindfold and began to tell us what the experiment had felt like to him. He admitted that he was beginning to get agitated by the horse's behavior. He hadn't noticed when it began, but it had started to get on his nerves right before I paused the experiment. He also could not believe how spending time on a farm with a horse had brought up the feelings of concern and indecision he was feeling at work. I congratulated him on keeping the blindfold on and he laughed. He had really, really, wanted to pull it off.

I asked them both to take a moment and thank one another for being such good guides. They had done an admirable job of communicating and keeping one another safe. And they admitted to each other what a marvelous job they each had done as guide. It was heartwarming to watch.

We gave them an opportunity to say their thanks to Lakota before Laurie led her back to her paddock. I noticed how they were both very present in their bodies. They were no longer reserved in stroking her neck and told her earnestly how glad they were to have met her. Her large eyes were relaxed and she received their praise quietly. We all took our seats back in the shade of the tree and rehydrated. They were excited about the whole experience.

The husband related that even as they finished the obstacle course, he had already gained insight into how he wanted to approach the work situation. He had a new understanding of it and was ready to take responsibility for his part in the scenario that had been unfolding. There were boundary issues around work, and work versus friendship, as well as other major ingredients being sifted through.

They both had loved the experiment and how well they had participated. They had no idea what to expect, but it had been even more powerful than they had hoped. So many things came up for them, individually and as a team, and they shared for quite a while. They told me they had one beautiful small child and had just found out they were expecting their second. They were concerned that they would not have the same degree of love for their new baby. They were also concerned about the challenges another being would bring to their wonderful life. But this afternoon together had shown them that they had the ability to face the situation together and work through whatever issues might come up. They were young and intelligent, and appeared to have a very healthy way of dialoguing. It was an honor to share this time with them.

When everyone left, I had the opportunity to spend time with my dear, sweet horse. I told her again how magnificent she had been. We contemplated how successful the afternoon had been as we both munched on carrots, our special treat.

There was no way I could have taught this beautiful horse how to do what she did that afternoon. We did not practice or rehearse. Just as every horse lives in the moment, I had to be in the moment to work with Lakota. I had no way of knowing what my clients would bring that day. I never know. And even if a client believes they know what they have come to work on, what actually comes up is often something else. My job as an equine coach is multifaceted and many of the facets need polishing at exactly the same moment. I have to be tuned in to my clients while observing my horse, interpreting the communication between them and my horse, and remaining open to guidance. When I receive guidance, I must choose whether to follow it or not, and if so, how.

I never see myself as doing this work by myself. I have always believed in guardian angels and see them as part of my higher guidance team. I have no proof, but I believe Lakota's guardian angels are with us also. After all, she may be receiving guidance, too, and it certainly is not coming from me. Or maybe it is her inherent talent at reading the energy of the client—that which is hidden deep within them, possibly so deep that they are unaware of it themselves. Whatever it is, you cannot fool a natural healer horse.

Lakota has certainly taught me patience. She has taught me about trust and friendship, stamina and stubbornness. And I continue to learn the fine points of communication from her.

This horse is a master teacher, a true sentient being, and I am a better person for having her in my life.

In my wildest dreams, I could never have imagined where we would end up all these years later. And the journey continues.

Annette Price is a storyteller, a businesswoman, a folkloric herbalist, and a lover of horses, sunshine, and life on this beautiful planet. She is a Missouri farm girl who morphed into a seeker of inner wisdom with the aid of celestial guidance and wondrous earthly friends. She graduated as an EGCM coach in 2011, founded On The Wings of a Horse coaching practice, and has been observing the healing gifts that horses offer during sessions with clients. This led to her new passion, the Healing Horse Registry International, whose mission is to collect, explore, and document empirical knowledge about this emerging healing modality.

Annette Price @ Dragonfly Farm
Certified Equine Gestalt Coach
www.onthewingsofahorse.com
www.healinghorseregistryinternational.com

Playing God

Ashara Morris

As a student in the Equine Gestalt Coaching Method program, I got to play God. No, not in the sense of playing God with another person's life. What I experienced had nothing to do with manipulation, power over another, or getting my own way. I never imagined I would actually be playing God, and in a way that had an incredible impact on me. But then, the coaching program has been full of surprises, all of them increasing my personal growth on a massive scale. And those gift-wrapped ah-ha moments have allowed me to access that most important of characteristics: heart. How ironic that I named my business Harmony's Heart Farm when I was struggling with living from my heart. Then again, perhaps it was my heart gently tap-tap-tapping a message from inside the box where it had been placed years ago, and I had finally started to listen.

As a child, I had dreamed of doing some sort of work that involved horses. Or maybe, I thought, I could be a psychologist, helping people with their issues. I loved talking with the horses. I not only anthropomorphized horses, but all the other many-legged brethren on the planet and those without legs at all. It didn't matter if it had fur, wings, or fins, they were my friends. Of course, that was met with skepticism and derision by many, so as I got older, I went more into my head about the animals, and especially horses. I thought of them less often as friends and more often as "animals." As so often happens, the older I got, the more dug in I got with earning a living, and the dream to work with horses or help people took a backseat to life. Even though I had horses, rode horses, and trained horses, I had forgotten about partnering and working with horses. That required heart, of which I had lost sight.

Then I heard about Touched by a Horse. Work with horses; partner with horses. Those were concepts that touched a deep-seated, long dormant desire. I looked into the program and knew there was something there for me. I had become so adept at keeping myself emotionally distanced from the horses, those tellers of truth. Still, my closed-off self knew this program could give me what I wanted—a lovely career hanging out in the barn with the horses. What I hadn't counted on was being blown wide open and coming out the other end a totally different person from the one I had been bandying about most of my life.

My mother had told me more than once that when I was growing up, she never know what I was thinking or feeling. I've always found that puzzling, because I spent most of my childhood feeling as though my heart were on my sleeve and that everybody knew *everything* I was thinking. And that was a scary thing. So much emotion, just below the surface! Apparently I was a lot better at hiding my feelings than I thought. Crying, or even strong emotion, was not popular with my family. When things got emotional for me, I escaped into my own little made-up world and put on the persona of someone I admired. It was easier than being myself. That persona could handle what was going on. That persona was usually someone bright, chipper, and "together." And that persona firmly grasped the heart on my sleeve, stuck it in a box, and locked the cover, nice and tight.

This duality of personality, the persona me and the real me, was very apparent to the horses. I had my very first round pen session during a weekend called a CORE, as part of our Touched by a Horse training. During the session, I was the client being coached by a more senior student, and it involved some lovely moments of connection with the horse, a wise gentleman named Shadow. It also involved an equal amount of time with Shadow blowing me raspberries from the other side of the round pen. My perky, upbeat facade wasn't fooling him for a minute. "Get real, and I'll come over there," he would mutter, lifting his tail in my direction. We tangoed all over the round pen, me struggling with hanging onto what had worked in the past, and he letting me know, kindly but in no uncertain terms, that what had worked for me up to this point was not the kind of relationship he wanted to have with me. All that perky protection I had learned as a child was going exactly nowhere in his world.

With all of the persona wearing and heart protecting going on, it might seem that my childhood was a horror, and that is not true. It was actually what might be considered normal. We laughed, we did things together, and we looked pretty good, I'm sure. From my post-certification viewpoint, though, I can see we were "in control," not real. There were so many unspoken things. And growing up in that environment, it was easy to box up my heart and keep it hidden. Shadow, and all his brothers and sisters, were having none of that. If I wanted to partner with them, I had to open my heart and let them in. I had to be willing to accept the pain of loss with the joy of being in their company. They were asking a lot.

Both as a young adult and as one entering middle age, I had a hard time sustaining a human relationship. They would last maybe four years and I'd move on. I never completely committed myself. I was great at beginnings, lousy at sustaining. No heart, you see. Nobody was going to get into my heart. Not even me. I was terrified of the feeling, of that place in all of us that touches a source beyond what we see here on the physical plane. The higher self, the All That Is. Some call it God. I called it . . . well, I didn't call it anything because I wouldn't look at it. I skirted around it. I gave lip service to it. I acknowledged it existed, but I wouldn't touch it.

As I got older, I took courses to help me improve on a personal level, and they helped, but the door to my heart had very sturdy hinges and a good lock. It would swing open a teeny bit and then snap shut the moment I felt the least bit vulnerable. I met and married a wonderful man who stood by me while I flailed and tried to run. And then I finally just had to stop the running because he understood his heart, and he stood in the chaos I created like a rock until I figured out that he loved me no matter what, without judgment. The box around my heart softened, but it tenaciously held on in other parts of my life.

It's no wonder I was afraid of having a heart attack and dying. Even though I had done a lot of work around opening my heart, I was still at odds with All That Is. If I couldn't touch or look at the basis of us all, how could I be comfortable with my own beating heart, that which we so often describe as the expression of that basis?

So there I was, the closed-hearted student, sick and tired of being constantly afraid, and finally ready to do whatever it took to push myself past all the garbage and get real. No more persona. Time to start living. Time to open the heart box. Umm, really?

The first thing I learned about myself over the ensuing months was the fact that I was not as bright and chipper and put together as I thought. Underneath that "can do" exterior was an introverted, supersensitive individual who kept her heart in a box and a smile on her face, afraid to speak her mind because someone might not like her and afraid to open her heart because, heaven forbid, someone might break it.

Remember Shadow and his raspberries? Thank goodness he was totally disinterested in the chipper persona and wanted someone genuine.

For one who was so closed but who thought herself quite open, being in the program was a revelation. I can remember going to my very first CORE, the weekend intensives where we practice and do our own personal work. I hung back a bit, observing, and was moved by the life experiences revealed during each piece of work. Boy, these people really had stuff to release! I remember saying in the closing circle that I was so very happy to be there, and that it was great, it was going to continue to be great, but gee, I felt like I had nothing on which to work. Everything was peachy in my little world. How chipper of me. Oh, how little I knew!

CORE after CORE, the layers were peeled away and oh, so slowly, the heart was revealed. The horses helped to make it bearable. QT, a feisty, opinionated, and gorgeous Paint, taught me to play and to "be." I was intimidated by him. His power can fill a stadium, and he has amazing presence. But once I allowed myself to look at him with my heart instead of my head, he showed me just how much fun it can be to relate to that much power. His power was all from the heart; it is always that way with the horses. Look deeply into their eyes and behold the power of total knowing. They stand in their heart and make no excuses. They are a wonderful embodiment of All That Is.

With each bit of learning and each revelation inspired by the horses, I became a little more comfortable with All That Is. I started looking at All That Is out of the corner of my eye. I was able to interact with my herd mates in a real way and not feel threatened by their beauty, intelligence, and openness, because little by little, I realized that I am beautiful, I am intelligent, and I can be open without fear of repercussion. Crying is okay. Laughing is okay. Even having a hissy fit is okay.

The pendulum swings broadly from side to side, from hysteria to total control, and in the center, at the very core of what we are, is the heart.

Because no human is exactly like another, we are drawn to some, repelled by others, and in many cases, neutral towards another. However, if we look deep inside, in each of us is All

That Is, that essence of which I was so afraid. The depth of emotion was, to me, overwhelming. There wasn't enough space inside me to hold it. Finding it in others was often a challenge, too, especially the ones for which I felt no affinity. Perhaps because it felt like such an intimate emotion and relationship to me, I struggled to see it in the people who, for whatever reason, irritated me. It was still there, though, that beautiful spark, that thing we call love. And I realized that if I opened myself to the compassion found in that spark, worlds dance together.

The horses teach this every day. Their honesty in the face of every emotion, every piece of unreality, every blame that we place on them, is taken in, loved, and released. Is this not what we do with All That Is? We ask, cajole, blame, thank, and question, but do we ever feel what is being returned? It is unconditional. It is heart, pure and simple, and so elemental that the very thought of that much love being bestowed upon us was, for me, difficult to accept. I was not worthy of all that love, that heart. It overwhelmed me. It was only in working with the horses and finding my own core that I could begin to grasp what All That Is feels for us every day, always. And that is what brought me to playing God.

At my very last CORE, a fellow student was having serious issues with God. Her coach decided it might be a good idea if the student, whom I will call Joan, had a conversation with God—talk to God, tell God how she felt. A volunteer was requested. And there I was, she who had been looking at All That Is from the corner of her eye, raising my hand. And chosen.

I had only recently begun to explore the possibility of looking at All That Is from more than the corner of my eye, so I had only a vague idea about what would be required of me. However, I had stopped questioning my intuition on many things. If I had a feeling I should turn left while driving and I turn right instead, invariably something came up to tell me that a left turn might have been a better choice. So it was with raising my hand. It was not a conscious decision. I was compelled to volunteer. Somebody or something was gently prodding me in the back, letting me know another piece of the puzzle was about to fall into place.

To play God, I was placed on a mounting block. After all, God is above us, right? I stood there, in all my celestial glory, with, I am certain, angels and saints to the right and left of me, although they were unseen by the masses. I felt like all of the Sunday school drawings of God had been thrust upon me. I was pretty much in my head, ready to play my part in the gestalt experiment. There was me and there was Joan. And what Joan had to say wasn't pleasant. But I was God and I could take it.

Joan had plenty to say to God. She screamed. She sobbed. She shook her fist in my direction and ranted, telling God how unfair life was, that God was asking too much, that she didn't know why it had to be her that had this life and this really crappy job of being in service to others. Why couldn't God just leave her alone and let her have some normalcy? Why did God have to keep asking? I just stood there and took it all in, impassive, being what in my head was godlike.

Ah, my head. Such a place to be when playing God. Thoughts flitted around in the cavern of my head. Did God really hear us? My little God, at that point, was just that—miniscule. Listening, but maybe not hearing. I was still playing a part. From the door on my boxed-up heart swung a sign: Closed. Joan was being completely genuine in her intense emotion, and in the face of it, I reverted. I donned one of my personas. This one was labeled "God," the being who could take any form of abuse and be unaffected by it. The being who could also dish out the punishment when so inclined. Someone who had power over any situation. Despite all the progress I had made relating to my heart throughout my training, when the time came to throw away the locks and open the door wide, I got right in the way of the process.

Gradually, though, as Joan continued her dialogue, something happened. I remembered the horses, their wisdom, their acceptance, their heart, and their embodiment of All That Is. I recalled how they show us that we all have this tremendous gift to allow love, and heart, to flow through us, no matter the circumstance, be it joy, sorrow, anger, or pain. We all have an amazing capacity to heal others, and ourselves, if we will just love. As I felt the immensity of that thought, the door creaked open, just a crack. And from that small sliver of space, an incredible light shone forth. The energy hidden in that box was immeasurable, the brightness of a dozen suns. I mentally tried to pull back. "Too dangerous!" my psyche cried. But once the door had been cracked there was no stopping it. I finally stopped thinking and started feeling.

I could feel light and emotion pouring into the center of my body, from where I did not know. Another dimension? A higher plane of existence? Wherever it was, it filled me, and I was no longer the impassive, godlike creature playing a part. I was being directed by something bigger than me to be something bigger than a safe persona and a stump on a mounting block. I was touching the spark, the heart, and the love that surrounds and connects us all. The door to my heart flew open and I perceived the sudden brightness of love surging forth. It was all I could do to stand still.

Joan was tired; she was in despair. She was incredibly sad in her feeling of betrayal by her maker. She felt alone, tears of agony slid down her cheeks. And in that moment I knew that we are never alone. We all have, in our hearts, a cosmic love that transcends everything. And that love wanted Joan to know it had room for all the pain and a soft, sweet cushion of safety and love to enfold her. Standing above, standing by, being impassive was no longer acceptable. I was directed down from the dais to embrace the beautiful being in front of me with the love and light pouring forth from the universe. This, I realized, is where God was—not on some throne in a place high in the clouds, stroking his beard and watching us struggle. No, God, the All That Is, was right down in the trenches with us, his creation. In one swift second, I was swept down the stairs and into the arms of my herd mate, Joan, to join with the being who made us all. What a delicious environment we were provided! Compassion. Caring. Sweet protection. Love. *Heart.* It was all there, and more, for the taking, as much as we both needed, to heal our hearts and join in the universal dance.

I realized the exercise was not just for Joan; it was also for me. All That Is had waited patiently while I weaved my way through my life to this moment. My heart was thrown wide open and the door would never again be completely closed. It might try, in an effort to return to what was known, but that is not the way of the heart. If one will merely listen, one is compelled to forever expand, expand, expand with each gentle beat.

The horses feel the heart, and when I am in my heart, my horses respond in a magical way. We understand one another on a level that is felt rather than thought. Life flows, it sings, and even the mundane has beauty. I can look into the eyes of the beautiful Wilma, my partner in this work, and know that she has the wisdom and knowledge to heal even the hardest of hearts. I have experienced her patience, her magic, her knowing. Her heart is pure and she gives of it freely. What better example could I have of how to *be* love? She is the equine embodiment of All That Is.

Playing God gave me the capacity to open myself to something extraordinary, to allow vulnerability, trust, compassion, caring, and to know that I am always loved, and that we are all love. It is not necessary to go through our lives feeling as though we have to do it ourselves. There is joy in every moment, even those that seem to be the worst of our lives. If we open our heart to All That Is, we know. We are never alone.

Ashara Morris walked like a horse before she walked like a person, much to the embarrassment of her Midwest family. She also carried on lively conversations with the family dog, cats, and even the small woodland animals she encountered on walks through the forest. After being sidetracked for a while by making a living, Ashara found her way back to her horse and animal roots, culminating in certification as an Equine Gestalt Coach in the Touched by a Horse EGC Method. Her practice is a sort of animal e-harmony, where she works with people to discover the best of themselves. They, in turn, can then bring their best to their beloved animal friends, especially animals who have been rescued and suffer from Post-Traumatic Stress Disorder (PTSD). It's all about L-O-V-E.

Ashara Morris
Certified Equine Gestalt Coach
Harmony's Heart Farm™
ashara@harmonysheartfarm.com
www.harmonysheartfarm.com

You See My Secrets

BB Harding

I looked into your eye
And my soul quivered
You saw something I have
Always failed to see
And you noticed it right away–
Was it a sadness that I have
Always hidden from others?
Was it a shame I never
wanted to wear?
Was it a brilliance I have
Never declared?
You looked into my soul
And I knew I would never
Be the same.

BB Harding is the owner of A Horse and a Wizard, which offers sessions combining Neuro-Integration and EGCM coaching.

BB Harding
www.ahorseandawizard.com
bb@ahorseandawizard.com

Internal Shifts

Heather Kirby

Of the hundreds of pieces of work I've seen, the most perfect example of the Equine Gestalt Coaching Method was the one most personal to me. It was also undoubtedly one of the most unimpressive to watch. To the innocent observer, there was simply a woman in a large round pen, walking with a horse and uttering only two or three sentences. However, what those observers couldn't see was the mountain that surely moved within me. And that is what the EGCM does: it moves mountains internally. It causes a shift that occurs on a mental, physical, spiritual, and cellular level that changes the course of your life forever. Sometimes the shift is evoked by a loud and dramatic piece of work, but sometimes the shift occurs quietly, even imperceptibly, within the soul.

It was my very first weekend workshop, and I really didn't know much about the EGC Method. All I knew was that Melisa was the kind of mentor I wanted. She had a solid clinical background but worked outside the box, incorporated horses, connected with clients, and did it all with integrity. So when she asked for a volunteer to demonstrate the method called "Reflective Round Pen," I volunteered, knowing nothing about what I was getting myself into.

Melisa asked me to step into the pen when I was ready. She described "ready" as having no attachment to what the horse would do . . . none whatsoever. She said that when I was fully grounded I would not be looking to connect with the horse or wanting the horse to seek me out, and I would have no agenda. I stood outside that pen for quite a while wondering what the heck it meant to "ground myself" and wondering if I would ever lose the desire to connect with that beautiful animal in the pen. I also wasn't sure I was capable of truly losing my agenda. Melisa talked me through it—how to feel the earth under my feet, how to get in tune with my body, and how to center myself. And I eventually felt like I could walk into the pen and be at peace with whether the horse approached me or not. Losing my agenda with the horse turned out to be easier than losing the jitters I had about being in front of strangers watching me. I felt self-conscious and nervous and had no idea what was going to happen. But I had a keen sense of curiosity and a deep sense of trust in the process, so I took a deep breath and just relaxed into the experience.

Melisa told to me to be in the pen in whatever way was comfortable for me. A highly energetic person, who rarely sits still, I began to walk around the pen. The horse was on the left side of the pen and appeared completely disinterested in me. I found myself walking on the outer right edge of the pen, clockwise from twelve to six, and then cutting directly across the middle, somewhat to avoid approaching the horse and somewhat because it felt natural. As I walked this half-moon pattern, I fell into a bit of a rhythm that felt similar to the walking meditation I often did in the woods back home. It was a rhythmic walk, a slow and steady pace which helped clear my head, open my heart, and left me feeling reflective, introspective, and at peace.

As I was walking, Melisa asked me if "anything was coming up." Not a person to divulge much among strangers, I simply nodded. She asked me to describe what was coming up and I simply replied that I was thinking about a relationship that I was in at the current time. She said to continue walking and thinking about the relationship and to be aware of my body, my thoughts, and my emotions. As I walked, I held in my mind this new, but intense, relationship. It was a relationship with lots of highs and lows. I had high hopes and grave concerns. I was not convinced the relationship was good for me, but wasn't ready to break it off either. As I continued to walk, I felt confusion and sadness. I felt tears well up behind my eyes. Then I sensed this huge, powerful being coming towards me from behind. I continued to walk and the horse continued to approach. Within a few minutes, I could feel his presence directly off my right shoulder. The exhilaration and awareness I felt in that moment changed everything.

In that moment I faced a choice: to continue to walk on the path I had created in the pen, in this rhythmic pattern in which I had felt centered, reflective, grounded, at peace, very attuned to my own journey . . . or to turn and face this amazing and powerful animal. I realized that often in my life when

I find myself at such a crossroads, I've turned away from my path. I have left my own path to embrace a person, a place, or a job that held so much magnetic appeal that it drew me in with the seductive offer of giving me something that I couldn't find for myself. But this time I felt so grounded, so at peace with walking the simple path around the pen that I wanted to continue. The magnetic pull toward integrity was stronger than the seductive pull of excitement. It felt like a test, but also like a gift. It felt like an opportunity and a moment of truth. And in that moment of truth, I chose to remain on my own path. As I continued my walking meditation, I was surprised that the horse having *not* received my attention, having not steered me from my path, began to walk along my path *with* me just off my inside shoulder. The feeling this evoked is hard to express. I felt an immense peace, a connectedness. I felt a partnership that I had never felt in my whole life. I felt that I was walking on my own path and being joined by an amazing and powerful being, walking *next* to me . . . not in front of me, not behind me, but *next* to me on my path and seeming to be finding its *own* path alongside mine.

When I came to the point in the round pen where I had previously cut across the circle, I faced another moment of truth. Do I avoid this being that is now going to be right in my way? I will surely run into him if I turn to the inside. Or do I stay on my path? At many similar junctures when some-one has gotten too close, or when something has felt too good, I have steered from the path. I have avoided that which seemed too wondrous, too magnificent, doubting that I was worthy, questioning if it was real, afraid to set myself up for disappointment. But at that moment I had a sense that I needed to stay on my own path. And if something wondrous was right smack in my path, I would embrace it. So as I turned, I moved toward the horse for the first time. Suddenly we were together, facing one another, our paths having literally crossed. Our eyes locked and my heart softened. I felt a strange and deep connectedness that I would later learn was called "contact." I gently reached up toward him and he bent his head down toward me. I felt a connection with this animal that could only be described as a soul connection. And in my heart I felt the horse speak with wisdom, "Remain on your own path and be open to true partnership."

The rest of the session is a bit of a blur. I remember feeling completely absorbed by the exchange with this horse and then suddenly hearing Melisa say, "Ok, the love fest is over . . . why don't you keep walking?" I walked on and the horse walked with me. And I remember Melisa asking me if I had any thoughts to share. I said, "Yes. I realize that I need to let go of my current relationship and stay on my own path." It was such a simple statement and I am sure that to those watching, who had seen dream work and psycho drama earlier in the workshop, it seemed very benign, possibly even a little boring compared to other pieces we had witnessed. But that simple and quiet piece shifted everything in my life. That one experience engrained in me a sense of integrity deeper than I had ever known and a sense of openness, more than I had ever felt, to the idea of a true partnership.

Following that weekend, I did end the relationship that I was in with someone who, while wonderful in many ways, was not appreciative of me, did not recognize my gifts, or honor my path and did not offer the kind of partnership that

I really wanted. It would be over a year before I would find such a partnership. But in that time I maintained a sense of peace knowing I was on my path and I was open to true partnership. I felt confident it would come if I remained on my path as it did that day in the round pen.

Since that first weekend workshop, I have seen so many examples of Equine Gestalt Coaching and many of them quite dramatic. Many of them with horses doing truly unbelievable things that almost defy reason. I've seen people release years of pent-up rage and deep, dark sorrow. I have heard people speak a truth never before spoken and seen relationships change in dramatic ways. However, my first piece of "personal work" remains the truest example to me of the EGC Method. For me it holds an important reminder that regardless of what it looks like from the outside, what truly matters is what happens *within* a person when they connect with the soul of a horse and receive an important personal message. What might appear small from the outside might inspire a significant shift in a person. As I have moved from student to practitioner of the EGC Method, that simple piece grounds me in the basics. It reminds me that if I assist my client in grounding themselves, create a space for the horse to work, and truly trust the process, my client will receive the message meant for them. The piece might look big or boring, but when a person connects with a horse, their reality changes forever. I know mine did.

Heather Kirby is a Licensed Clinical Social Worker, a Certified Substance Abuse Counselor, and holds a master's degree in Special Education. She has spent over twenty years working directly with children, adolescents, and families in a variety of mental health and special education settings. She specializes in reaching difficult teens through alternative therapies and has created her own activity-based therapeutic approach called Facilitated Socialization™. She was the first graduate of Melisa Pearce's certification program in the Equine Gestalt Coaching Method and has completed the advanced training in Trauma-Focused Equine Assisted Psychotherapy with Tim and Bettina Jobe. In 2011, Heather was recruited to develop an equine therapy program for Childhelp, a national organization providing residential treatment for children of traumatic abuse and neglect. The position allowed her to combine her passion for equine therapy with her skills as a clinician and her talent for program development. Currently, Heather works in private practice with offices in Bethesda, MD, and Fairfax, VA, and provides equine therapy through a partnership with Project Horse, Inc. in Purcellville, VA.

Heather Kirby, LCSW
Kirby Creative Clinical Solutions, LLC
www.KCClinicalSolutions.com

Zoey, the Super Pony

Chantel Schmidt

My journey to finding my horse partner started many years before she came into my life. My path to her was a long road, much like my path to healing.

In my twenties, I suffered a silent affliction. My self-defeating thoughts about my body had taken a grip over my happiness. At the time, I had two small children and was living on a dead-end road in the middle of nowhere. I was left with many hours to think, and think I did. It didn't matter how busy I was as a mom, my thoughts where there. I looked into the mirror several times throughout the day to find something I didn't like in the reflection. People around me told me how beautiful I was, which only made things worse for me because that just created more pressure to live up to a certain image. From what I could see, I wasn't worthy of the flattering comments. My focus was on all the imperfections I thought I had. Surprisingly, I was able to keep up a façade of having everything together. But on the inside, I was living a nightmare.

One of my favorite places to escape to during this time was my Uncle Wally's place, a place where thoughts about my body didn't haunt me. My uncle was old, and I felt safe in knowing he truly accepted me no matter what. He never commented on how pretty I was. We would just spend countless hours discussing my favorite subject: horses. Wally raised Quarter Horses and Paints. It was at Wally's that I fell in love with a horse named Spook. Jet black, with a snow white blaze and four white socks, Spook was beautiful beyond words. She was my dream horse. Her coat was so black that it had a purple hue, and she glistened and shone like the sun itself. I knew I had to own her. It took almost a year to finish paying my uncle for Spook, but she was finally mine.

But Spook wanted nothing to do with me, and each time I went to ride her, Spook acted like she had never seen a saddle before. She was unpredictable. Even worse, she started living up to her name: she was scared of everything. She got worse every year and eventually could not be ridden.

I had been cautioned by my uncle and others not to buy Spook, but I kept her for thirteen years, hoping that everyone was wrong and that somehow, she would turn out to be the horse for me. Everywhere I went with her, people commented on how striking she was, which made me even more determined to keep my gorgeous horse.

It's no surprise that I was focused only on the looks of the stunning Spook. For over twenty years, I had struggled with a weight obsession. From the time I woke up until the time I went to sleep, my weight was all I thought about. Some nights I dreamed about my body. How I looked in the mirror was my focus; what the scale said dictated my day. It got so bad that I didn't want to go anywhere because of how I believed I looked. Like any obsession, it got worse as the years went by. I knew it was time to deal with the turmoil going on inside, but even though I began to realize that I was a mess, I wasn't sure how to change. Living outside my body had become normal for me. I was completely disconnected; my thoughts became my reality. I kept going back to what I knew: diets, self-loathing, and looking for the next quick fix.

Every year that went by, Spook got worse, and eventually, she could no longer be ridden. No wonder poor Spook got worse year after year. I had focused my obsession with looks on to my horse. She wanted nothing to do with this craziness. Who could blame her?

A woman responded to the advertisement I took out on Spook and asked if I would trade her for an untrained Buckskin filly. She wanted to raise black-and-white Paints. Spook would become a broodmare for her. In terms of price, what she offered as a trade was by no means comparable. To this day, I'm not sure why I agreed to the trade, but something inside just said yes. My ego justified the trade by telling me that I could train this little filly and resell her.

I didn't want to give up on Spook, yet I knew I couldn't continue on the same path with her. I wasn't sure how this new horse was going to fit into my life. I had mixed feelings as I sat in the yard waiting for her to arrive, and my stomach was full of butterflies as I watched them pull up the driveway. We handed each other the ropes of our new horses. Spook jumped in the trailer while I walked away with Zoey. The trade was quick, like ripping off a Band-Aid®. There was no point to prolonging the pain. I watched them drive away wondering if I had made a mistake. I was sad to see my dream horse go, but a new horse meant a new life and I felt an instant connection with Zoey.

Saying good-bye to Spook was a pivotal moment for me. I started to consider that there might be more to me than what the eye could see.

At first, I focused on imperfections and picked Zoey apart the way I did myself. Very quickly, those "imperfections" faded away. Zoey actually enjoyed being with me. She accepted me and the love I gave her. I felt that, just maybe, I had found the horse I needed. Zoey seemed wise beyond her years. When I was with her, I felt a deep connection. She saw through my darkness and into my light. Somehow she got through to a place in me that had been locked and guarded. Slowly, my wall started to come down with Zoey's help. She was helping me heal from past hurts. Just being with her, brushing her, and listening to her chew as she ate the grass was therapy for me.

I typically started riding a horse within three days of her arrival, but this time it was different. I was in no rush to get on and ride Zoey. This horse was different and so was the experience. I spent many days just hanging out with this magnificent healer and getting to know her. I would lay in the sun holding her rope as she grazed in the yard. I even let her loose, knowing she wouldn't leave. This was something I had wanted for years, but when I had tried it with Spook, she was off like a flash of lightning. My faith in Zoey grew each day. It was good to trust again, and it felt good to have a horse that not only received my love, but also gave it back. She didn't run from me, she came to me. Spook had shown me my inside monster while Zoey saw past that to the wounded soul in need of nurturance.

When the time came to start Zoey's training, I decided it would be best to send her to someone else. The years with Spook, combined with a few bucking incidences with other horses, had gotten me a little jumpy. I wasn't going to attempt anything that would ruin the good thing I had going with Zoey. She did really well at the trainers and she never offered to buck, which was a huge relief for me.

I was really excited the day I picked Zoey up from the arena. I watched the trainer ride her around and Zoey looked great. Then it was time for me to try. I rode her around while the trainer watched. As I was riding, the trainer warned me that Zoey would buck if I kicked too hard or used spurs. Out came a whole list of things *not* to do. To say I was confused is an understatement. Thoughts ran through my head. The trainer had said she'd never bucked. Was there something she wasn't telling me? This didn't seem likely because I was sure she wouldn't hide something like that from me. It took me a few weeks to realize the trainer was reflecting my own thoughts.

I was a little scared to get on Zoey at home, but I trusted her. The problem was that I didn't trust myself. I knew I needed to face and deal with my fear, and I wasn't going to let my fear stop me from getting in the saddle. But Zoey had a different idea. She wouldn't budge. I tried everything I knew, but nothing worked. I was stumped when Zoey just quietly turned and sniffed my boot, refusing to move forward. At first I found her boot sniffing comforting, but as time went on, I was less entertained. I left those moments frustrated, wondering why Zoey wasn't going forward. Day after day, there was no movement. I tried different saddles, different bits, different cues. Nothing seemed to motivate her to move forward. I knew, deep down, that Zoey was telling me something about me and my life. This was the most frustrating thing of all.

One day, Zoey was following me around as I walked amongst the herd, coming up behind me and giving me gentle nudges on my back. At first I thought this was cute. Maybe she wanted attention. But when she gave me a big push, her message became clear.

I looked at her and said, "Okay, I get it. I'm stuck."

As soon as I acknowledged this to her, she quit pushing on my back and quietly walked behind me. I wasn't moving forward in life and Zoey was letting me know it. I was discontent, wanting to do something more in my life, but I wasn't moving forward with anything. I was stuck with my ideas, stuck with my body image, stuck in my life, and stuck in the mud!

Zoey's push gave me the momentum I needed to start my search for something I would love doing. I awoke each morning asking myself a simple question: What do I love to do? My immediate answer was that I love to be with horses and that helping people filled my heart with joy. If only I could make a living at those things!

I got to work, researching many programs. I was looking into equine assisted therapy, equine assisted learning, and basically anything that involved horses helping people. After a year of searching, I finally found the perfect fit. My friend had found a program on the Internet and told me to check it out. I talked to the owner, Melisa Pearce, and asked a few questions. Most importantly, I took time to sit with it to feel whether or not it was the "right" one. On the day of the enrollment deadline, I decided to go ahead with the program. I really had no idea what I had signed up for, but I jumped in, ready to find out.

I started studying the EGC Method at Touched by a Horse in July 2011. I live without regret for joining this life changing program, and I would do it again in a hoof beat. Around the time I started the program, I decided to pick up a book by Marianne Williamson titled *A Course in Weight Loss*. What a true journey to healing I had begun. I had been on many diets and read some good books before, but not like this. This one dealt with the internal issues around my weight. I thought I had already dealt with all the past pain, but boy, was I in for a surprise.

It was September when I made it to my first of the eight required CORE weekends for the EGC method. It was the very first Canadian CORE, and I was happy to have it close to home. I found out very quickly how little I really knew about what I had jumped into. I had to do personal work? The deep inner torment had to come out? I was nervous, but it didn't feel as scary knowing that I could spill my pain and have a horse there to support my tears. The horses showed up in a big way for me that weekend, as did all the other "herd members." Yes, I was part of a herd of incredible people, with an outstanding leader. I felt the support not only from the four-legged partners, but from everyone there.

At this particular CORE, I got to watch several horses being assessed for the capacity to coach. Melisa did not know the horses and was checking to see what the horses' "gift" might be. I watched one horse, Ricky, do exactly what we were conveying through our thoughts. I have always known horses were telepathic, but this was beyond anything I could have imagined. Ricky mirrored my thoughts and those of two other students. When the third student attempted to communicate with Ricky, something quite amusing happened. She explained to us that she wanted him to go to the right around the pen and stop at the gate. Ricky went around the pen instantly and stopped at the gate, but he went to the left, not the right. All of us were confused and thought he had gone the wrong way. It took us a while, but eventually we figured out that Ricky had actually done exactly what she wanted because even though she told us she wanted him to go right, she was visualizing Ricky going to the left.

I left my first training a little mystified, but I couldn't wait to try it with my horses. Wow! I couldn't wait to go back and learn more.

Each time I went to a CORE, the horses did something I had never seen before. I quickly began to understand why I felt so good when around my horses. Horses actually have the capacity to heal. Chakras were something I knew nothing about until this program. Watching horses work on certain parts of the human body helped me gain knowledge of the chakra system.

My jaw nearly hit the arena floor as I watched one of Melisa's horses, Abhainn, a magnificent Gypsy Vanner, work on a student in the round pen. As Abhainn walked up to the student and started moving his head methodically up and down her right arm, his lips made a smacking sound. I could almost see him sucking stuck energy from her shoulder. Melisa explained that Abhainn was doing a physical healing. He continued moving up and down this student's arm. As he moved towards her chest, Melisa cautioned him not to smack the girl in the head. Abhainn immediately slowed his pace as he continued to work his magic. I just sat there in awe; I wouldn't have believed it if I hadn't seen it with my own eyes. The student had an injury on her arm and Abhainn knew exactly where healing was needed. I was in tears after watching this beautiful moment.

During my CORE weekends, I was doing some very deep personal work. Meanwhile, at home, I was listening to the *A Course in Weight Loss* CDs. Slowly but surely, my inner critic started to show up less and got quieter. At first, it was hours without hearing from her, then days, and then weeks. I stopped getting on the scale and started speaking kind words to myself and my body. I was able to see my true value for the first time, and it had nothing to do with my outward appearance. There was more to life than my physical body. I finally put down the beating stick and showed up for my life.

The time came for me to begin practicing my EGCM work. I started to see clients for exploratory sessions and Zoey showed her ability to coach in many ways. She was even picking up on clients' energy before they arrived at my home. While waiting for one client to arrive, Zoey would run and buck, kicking her legs wildly around the round pen. This wasn't typical of Zoey, but being new to this method, I just thought it was strange. I remember her looking at me as if to say, "Really, you don't get it?"

As our client drove up the driveway, Zoey went off bucking and kicking furiously again. Body somatics is an important part of the EGC Method, and through further exploration with the client, I realized that his heart was racing. I asked him to put words to how fast his heart was and he compared his heart to a Mustang sports car driving on a bumpy road. Zoey's wild activity could also be compared to a fast car on unsteady terrain. She was imitating what was happening with the client.

"All about YOU" was the name of the first workshop I held at my place. Zoey is usually the first one in the herd to put her hoof up to coach, and this day was no exception. She was ready and waiting in the pen. Zoey came right to the gate to greet her clients, ears perked intently, listening to every-thing that was said. It was a windy day, which made it difficult to get settled in. Even though papers were flying everywhere, Zoey seemed to be unfazed by all the distractions. I trusted her completely. Once we were finally ready to explore, I brought a client into the round pen.

The client, Norma, was having difficulty with a long-time friend. Very hurtful things had been said and Norma was at a loss for how to handle the situation. This seemed to be a pattern in this particular friendship. Zoey followed Norma lovingly around the round pen as Norma was trying to figure out how to handle the situation with her friend. After walking around, thinking about solutions to the problem, Norma stopped and stood still. At this point, Zoey went up to Norma and started to work on chakra balancing her. As Zoey focused on Norma's throat chakra, I asked her if there was something she wasn't saying or something that she needed support in saying. Norma explained that her throat had a lump in it and she wasn't sure she could express her feelings. With that, Zoey sniffed down her leg, and nipped her. Norma immediately had lots to say. Zoey had cleared her throat chakra!

Zoey then got very affectionate with her, but Norma was visibly uncomfortable and trying to avoid her. Zoey kept trying, sticking her muzzle in Norma's face as Norma walked around holding her hands up, as if trying to protect herself. When I asked Norma if this felt similar to the situation with her friend, she stopped in recognition. Norma explained that her friend had attacked her out of the blue, just like Zoey had done with her bite. Her friend then wanted to kiss and make up, like Zoey nuzzling and putting her muzzle in Norma's face. Norma wasn't ready to trust this friend again, resistant and protecting herself, just like she had done with Zoey. Once acknowledged, Zoey stopped and just stood while Norma thanked her for the lesson learned. Today, Norma is much more aware of when she isn't using her voice. Something shifted energetically that day for Norma though her work with Zoey.

This great little mare has coached many other times since that day with Norma, but she has not offered to nip anyone. We had a talk and she has found other more subtle "horsey" ways, like chakra balancing and pantomime, to make her point with clients.

Long before I knew about the EGC Method, Zoey was already coaching me. I was the student and she the teacher. From the day I started on this incredible journey, Zoey has been willing to move forward for me. On the days I feel myself slipping back into the old pattern, I think about those frustrating days sitting in the saddle going nowhere. Zoey went to great lengths to show me how bad being stuck could be. It was her love that removed my fear.

What I have learned from Zoey is this: Pretty is as pretty does. It is the heart that matters. If I follow my heart, I will not go wrong. You can't force timing, but you can pick a direction and move. Live your truth, and don't get stuck in the mud.

It is in gratitude for Zoey that I write my tale. It is because of her that my life is well.

Chantel Schmidt has been in love with horses since she was a young child riding at her uncle's ranch. She spent her childhood competing in local shows and participating in 4-H Club, and at the age of twelve, she got her first horse. While raising her three children, Chantel spent eight years as a volunteer and instructor in 4-H and worked as a home healthcare aide.

Ten years ago, she and her husband of twenty years purchased their dream farm, where they have been training, raising, and enjoying horses ever since. As owner and founder of Equine Reflection, Chantel collaborates with horses to facilitate wellness for clients through a holistic approach. Utilizing the powerful Equine Gestalt Coaching Method developed by Melisa Pearce, she and her equine partners assist people in letting go of the past in order to gain bright new perspectives and transform their lives.

Chantel Schmidt
Founder, Equine Reflection
chantel@equinereflection.com
www.equinereflection.com
Bringing Understanding and Healing Through
the Spirit of a Horse

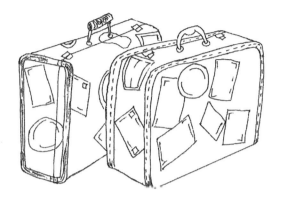

From the Winners Circle to the Round Pen

Jennifer Malocha

Ever since I can remember, I have wanted my very own human, someone I could belong to, someone who saw me as something more than a commodity or as a thing with a dollar sign on my forehead.

As far back as I can remember, I was taught that my job was to run—to run and to win. Truth be told, I loved to run and I loved to win! I was so good at it, in fact, that I ran for ten long years and I won close to $200,000 for my owners. I had 102 starts and placed in the top three in sixty percent of the races that I ran in.

Being a professional athlete took its toll on me physically. My body began to break down from the stress of the track. I began to feel all the injuries I had sustained over the years and I began to slow down. My owners kept me going by giving me drugs that masked the pain. After all, I had no value if I didn't win, and in order to win, I had to run.

I knew what happened to the horses that slowed down and were of no value because I had overheard a couple of grooms talking about it. They said that those horses were loaded onto a truck and sold for slaughter. I was scared of being sent away, so I kept running to postpone the inevitable.

I had so many owners that I lost count of the number, but it was over thirty. I was handled by many, many people—owners, trainers, exercisers, and grooms. Many people came and went in my life but I was never connected to them. I never even met some of my owners. No one ever stayed. Even though I was surrounded by people, I always knew that I was on my own. I learned how to be a survivor. My last owner was different than other track owners and he didn't send me to slaughter. Instead, I went into a pasture with some other horses.

One day a kindly woman came and took me and another horse to a barn away from our field. It turns out that the woman had really come to take the other horse and part of the agreement was that she had to take me, too, or she couldn't have the horse she wanted.

She was kind to me and did her best by me, but the trainer who owned the barn didn't like me. No one in this new place liked me and I missed my herd of racehorses. As time went on in the new barn, I felt the need to protect myself more and more. The barn owner hit me really hard with a lounge whip during training sessions. I became more and more frightened of the whip and my time with that man. I was locked in a twelve-by-twelve stall for days at a time and I became very aggressive to the humans in the barn. The day that I trapped a young girl in the corner of the arena was the day the barn owner told the kindly woman she had to put me down—he meant kill me—and said that if she didn't, he would.

I was locked in a stall until the day she found a place for me to go. Thank the Creator that she loved me enough to find a place for me to go. She loaded me into her horse trailer and we drove for what felt like forever. I got out of her trailer and was loaded into another one with a different woman. Again we drove for a long, long time.

When I came out of the trailer I was in a strange new place. I didn't trust this new human. As far as I knew she was just like the rest of them. I lunged at people who came near me, trying to bite them or strike them with my hooves. But I learned over time that this new woman was different. Her name was Monica and she really didn't want to hurt me. In fact, she wanted to help me. Monica was very kind, and I began to trust her a little bit more each day.

I had been living with Monica for about four months when she came into my life. The day started out just like any other day, and when I was brought into the arena I had no idea that this day would be the day my life would change forever.

A new woman came to meet me, and in that moment I knew that I had finally found My Girl—my very own human person! I saw into her heart, into her very soul. I saw her pain, her love, her strength, her weakness, her power. Most importantly, I could see in her the very thing I had longed for my entire life: my forever companion. When she reached out and touched me for the first time I felt the warmth of her touch. I felt the love she already felt for me in her gentle caresses. I knew that she would love me forever, just because. When it was time for her to go, I followed her to the gate. I could feel her uncertainty, but I could also feel that she fell in love with me that day too, and all I could do was hope that she trusted herself enough to take me home with her. I'll let her start telling some of the story now.

Lots of little girls dream of horses, but those dreams usually fade away over time. Not so for me. My desire never went away. As I grew older and my sons were getting close to leaving the house, my desire for an equine companion grew stronger. At the age of forty-three I started taking weekly riding lessons from a neighbor. After a year of lessons, I simply had to have my own horse. This was to be my first horse; I had never even leased a horse before. When I started my search, a dear friend tried to persuade me to buy what is called a school master, a really well trained horse, as my first horse. The universe had other ideas.

I believe in second chances, which is why I started looking at off-the-track Thoroughbreds. This was definitely not what my friend wanted me to get as my first horse. I met Teddy in February 2007 and my heart just knew that he was my horse. My heart recognized him as an old friend. I knew that Teddy was my horse because my heart recognized him. Even though I was told that he was overly aggressive, I recognized myself in him. I instantly understood him and knew that he was kind. I also knew that you can't train kindness into a horse but you can teach them everything else they need to know. What I didn't know until years later was that he would lunge at people trying to strike them and bite them. I found this surprising but understandable. I also used to be filled with rage because, like him, I had a lot to be mad about.

Very early in my life I learned how to read body language and hear the meaning behind spoken words. It helped me to gauge the severity of the storm I'd have to weather, and in some cases, it enabled me to turn the tide by being engaging, entertaining, and charming. This ability was what allowed me to see into Teddy's heart, into his very soul—to see who he really was. I knew he really didn't have much training and that he'd be a "project horse." At thirteen years old he had a body that was closer to twenty because of the toll his career as a professional athlete had taken on him. I knew little about horses and nothing about training. What I did know was that he was my horse. He needed to come home with me and spend the rest of his life as my pampered pony.

I also recognized that Teddy and I had a lot in common. We were both competitive athletes. We both had been abused. We both learned how to survive on our own. We both learned how to become fighters who could take care of themselves. We also both had huge hearts and a huge capacity for love and forgiveness. We were both born to be healers.

Teddy entered my life just as my oldest son was getting ready to head off to college. This is where even more fascinating parallels began to appear.

My husband and I were having serious problems in our marriage at the same time that I found a trainer to help me with Teddy. When I put Teddy into training with a young woman named Tanya, who was trained and mentored by

Buck Brannaman, I was not allowed to interact with Teddy at all except over the fence. I realized that I needed to do the same with my husband. By letting go of my need to try to fix everything and everyone else, I was able to start focusing on the person who needed my attention most—me.

Teddy began training with Tanya in September 2009, and in December of that year, due to a series of events, Teddy became so lame he could barely walk. I thought I was going to have to put him down. My husband, sons, and I went on a cruise right at that time. During the cruise, my oldest son said to me, "Mom, I really love you and I really love Dad, but the two of you would be better apart." He was right. It just wasn't working between us, so when we got home from the cruise, I made an appointment to start divorce proceedings.

On an emotional level, I prepared to let go of both the horse I had always dreamed of and my husband of more than twenty years. I loved them both with a great and burning passion, but realized that I needed to let go and begin to move forward. The funny thing is that within a week, my husband and I began to work to save our marriage and Teddy's lameness began to get better.

I spent many hours learning how to work with my horse, as well as learning how to actually ride. I also stepped away from my business to devote all my time and energy to rebuilding a life with my husband and our family.

Around December of 2010, I began to grow weary of the constant battle with depression that I had fought daily for most of my life. It was growing more and more challenging to keep my head above the waterline. The ironic thing is that I was the happiest and safest I had ever been in my entire life, which is probably the reason I fractured into a million pieces mentally. I was finally able to fall apart in a safe and loving space. During that time all I did was walk the dog, work on my horsemanship skills, and ride Teddy. I did a lot of personal healing work as well. When I was with Clyde T. Dog (my dog) or Teddy, I could be myself. They not only loved me, they loved all of me, even the broken and damaged bits.

Well, My Girl did indeed take me home with her despite the fact that she had a big, big job ahead of her. I could tell that she was pretty determined. From the very beginning I knew she wasn't afraid of me. For some reason, she trusted me not to hurt her.

She brought me to a barn and introduced me to a lady named Tanya. Tanya was a trainer, but not a trainer like I had experienced in the past. She always treated me fairly, was patient, and taught me how to connect the reins and her body to my feet. I had a great respect for Tanya, even though I pulled out all my old tricks that worked to scare all the other humans. She never missed a beat. She just kept asking for what she wanted and wouldn't stop until I gave it to her. She never got mad, she never lost her temper, and she was always fair. She even gave me lots of rubs when I tried my hardest. Those rubs made me want to try even harder.

During the time I was learning from Tanya, My Girl was learning from her too. Tanya didn't let My Girl work with me for a long time since I had so much to learn. She was concerned that My Girl would make too many mistakes and confuse me. I was really weak when we first started my training. I even fell over a few times because my muscles were weak. All that time I was locked in a stall was bad for me. But I grew stronger and stronger. I also began to realize that I could begin to trust the humans who were in my life now. Not one of them wanted to hurt me, and they were all trying their hardest to help me. I began to work really hard at doing what was asked of me.

My Girl would come and visit me, so I knew she still wanted me. I also saw Tanya teaching her how to communicate with horses the way Tanya did. My Girl was pretty clumsy for a long time. She also wasn't very good at riding horses. I could tell that she got frustrated, but she kept trying her hardest.

Then Tanya let My Girl work with me one day. It was such an exciting day! It didn't go very smoothly, but it was a beginning. No matter how frustrated My Girl got, she never got mad at me. In the beginning, I was always ready to fight back, to defend myself, but I never had to. I slowly began to understand that whatever mistakes were made, My Girl always thought they were her fault, which is why she never got mad at me. She got mad and frustrated with herself, but never with me.

Over time, I got the feeling that when she was very young, she learned how to take the blame for everything that went wrong, even the things that weren't her fault. I started being more tolerant and patient with her mistakes. I even started to fill in where she made mistakes in hopes that she would stop being so hard on herself.

We were both learning a lot. There were good days, there were bad days, and there were even a few great days. As we got to know each other better, I knew that she was afraid, even though she wasn't afraid of me. Then I figured out what was making her afraid. She was afraid that she wouldn't be able to stop me or support me if I got scared and tried to run away. She was afraid that her lack of knowledge and ability would end up letting me get hurt. When I realized what her fear was, it dawned on me that she might lose faith in herself and not keep me. That was a very bad day for me.

Thank goodness she loved me too much to not have me in her life. A little while later, she moved me to a new home. It was a place where I got to see her almost every single day. We began to go out for trail rides and even went riding in mountains. We've ridden in the Cascade Mountains and the Olympic Mountains. My Girl even took me to a place where she made me go in a river, and the river even had things she called salmon swimming in between my legs.

Over the years she's even taken me to meet Buck Brannaman a number of times. Thanks to him, we've really learned how to be a great team. Without him, I'm pretty sure I wouldn't be with My Girl anymore. My life has really changed thanks to My Girl. For most of my life, all I knew was how to go really fast around an oval, always to the left. Now I'm her Beloved Pony, and we get to have all sorts of adventures together!

In the spring of 2010, it was time to bring Teddy home from training. I was terrified! I wasn't afraid of what he might do, I was afraid that I wouldn't be able to handle what might happen. I had to make a choice. I could choose to get rid of

Teddy and get a new horse or I could choose to keep Teddy and just keep doing my best. I knew that not many people would want an off-the-track Thoroughbred with physical limitations, let alone one who needed a lot of training to be considered safe. The reality was, if I didn't step up and become the leader Teddy needed me to be, he would be put down. As scared as I was, I loved Teddy too much to give up and let that happen. I had no choice other than to be the leader he needed me to be. Period. From the day I decided Teddy was my horse, my learning curve has been straight up.

Many people have shared their "wisdom" with me under the guise of being helpful: I shouldn't have been allowed to get Teddy. He was too dangerous for me. He was beyond my ability. I needed to get a safer horse. What these people didn't know, what they couldn't possibly understand, was that I couldn't give up on Teddy. In a very real sense, giving up on Teddy would have meant giving up on me. If I gave up on Teddy, then there was no hope for me.

What these people also failed to understand was that Teddy was more than just a horse to me, he was the manifestation of my lifelong dream. But the most important thing they didn't realize was the depth of my determination to succeed. If I had to do it all over again, I'd still choose Teddy. But I was lucky. I met Tanya. Without Tanya the chance of our success as a team would have been somewhere between low and nonexistent. We were the ultimate long shot! And we were very fortunate. I've experienced so much healing, personal growth, and insight with Teddy's help. I am forever in his debt.

I began the Touched by a Horse, Equine Gestalt Coaching Method program created by Melisa Pearce in June of 2011. I knew the healing that Teddy had brought to me and I wanted to share it with others. What I didn't know when I started on the journey to get my certification is that I would be able to heal the pain inside me—pain I thought I'd take with me to my grave.

As I've alluded to, my childhood was filled with abuse: physical, mental, emotional, and sexual abuse, as well as abandonment and neglect. When I was twenty-three my best friend—my big brother and only sibling—was killed in a car accident. I have experienced a lot of trauma in my life and some wounds are harder to heal than others.

Before attending my first Touched by a Horse CORE training, I had decided not to use Teddy in the work because he is a supersensitive soul and I wanted to protect him. However, after I came home, I decided to try one of the healing exercises I had learned and in doing so, I discovered that Teddy is a master healer. His healing gifts are so profound that he astonished not only my first practice client, but me, too. In fact, one of my clients renamed him Teddy the Wonder Horse because of the powerful healing she experienced while working with him. The truly amazing thing is that he had never seen another horse do work of this kind. He just knew what to do and how to do it.

By using the horsemanship skills I learned from Buck Brannaman and Tanya, I was able to help Teddy process, heal, and drop the "baggage" he had carried for so long. And by helping him heal, I discovered that I healed some too. Sadly, some of my wounds were too deep even for Teddy to help me with. Under the loving guidance of Melisa Pearce, I was able to process, heal, and drop my own baggage. During the two years I trained to become a Certified Equine Gestalt Method Coach, I left a lot of that baggage in the sand of Melisa's arena. During that time I also learned many powerful healing techniques from Melisa, my very gifted teacher.

After a while, My Girl went away, but just for a little while. And she was different when she came back. She talked to me differently and I knew she could understand me even better than before. She began to bring people for me to "talk" to who were carrying their own baggage. I found that I could see into the hearts of the people she brought to talk to me. I could see their pain, I could see what was bothering them, and I just knew how to help them. It helped that My Girl had learned how to listen to me so she could help me explain things in human because I can't speak in a way that most humans can understand. My Girl seemed really happy and I got lots more carrotses than I normally got. I even got carrotses from the people that came to talk to me—and I love carrotses.

Now she brings more and more people to talk to me and we've really become a great team for helping these people heal and leave their baggage in our round pen. Recently she came out to the barn to share with me what people had told her about working with us. It made me feel really great to know that we had helped these people. They said that working with me had helped them release fear, set boundaries, connect with themselves in deep ways, and had given them profound peace.

One even said that I have a BS meter. I'm not sure I know what that means, but My Girl said that it is very good.

I love my new life, but what I love the most is My Girl. Every day I do my best to let her know just how much she means to me and how grateful I am for her. And every day I tell her that I will love her for the rest of my life.

Teddy used to be an overly aggressive, angry horse who has blossomed into an incredibly loving healer. I used to be an incredibly angry, distrustful woman who has blossomed into a peaceful soul who helps others find peace within themselves with the assistance of Teddy the Wonder Horse, my incredible equine healing partner.

In honor of my champion and his long racing career, I've done my best to put into race terms the powerful healing work we do as a team. I call it The Trifecta. In horse racing, the term trifecta means you correctly choose which horses will come in third (show), second (place) and first (win). In life, we are challenged with choosing a trifecta every day. The first thing we have to do is show up for our lives. We need to actually get ourselves to the starting gate. Then we have to find a place that is safe and conducive to healing. Finally, we have to become okay with winning—embrace it even. Once we can do all these things—show, place, win—we can heal our past and move on down the home stretch and into the winner's circle to enjoy the prosperity of the trifecta!

Jennifer Malocha started swimming and diving competitively when she was just six years old. She has played most every sport and completed sprint and Olympic distance triathlons. She has coached over two hundred women across the finish line of their first fitness events, including 25+ mile bike rides, triathlons, and open water distance swims. With her healing partner, Teddy the Wonder Horse, she helps her clients journey to depths they never knew they possessed to discover strengths they never knew they had. This empowers and teaches clients how to create and step into the life of their dreams. Her passion is to help people open their hearts to discover their passion, to help them see things in a bold new way, and to stretch farther than they ever thought they could. Jennifer believes the key to a truly happy and successful life is to strengthen and deepen communication and connection with oneself and others. She lives in Bellevue, WA, with her husband, their two sons, a dog named Clyde, and Teddy the Wonder Horse.

Jennifer Malocha
Wuhoo Coaching
jennifer@wuhoocoaching.com
www.wuhoocoaching.com

The Awaken Sonnet

Jennifer West

His eyes are that of liquid light
But they turn from me, ignored.
Connection is my only wish and so I fight
By stepping close, but he is bored.

The pain familiar I've held it strong
Aloud I speak my truth, uncaring all
The more I want, I chase, they run. This is my only song.
To connect, I long, I fail and I fall.

As my tears pour forth; awareness found
A wave of heat, a tingle on my back
Beside me now, a request not made, his need from me to ground
With his heart to mine I feel no longer black.

The lesson learned authentic forever I remain
My arms wrapped tight around his chest and face buried
in his mane.

Stated Outright

Jennifer West

My polarity is set for the group
In awareness my shoulders do droop
The horse makes it clear
Which direction he'd steer
When all that remains is a poop

Jennifer West graduated from the EGCM program in February 2013. She combines playful functional movement techniques with equine gestalt coaching to assist people as they reignite their fire for life.

Jennifer West
www.CaprioleCoaching.com

The Gift

Margo Green

It happened quite unexpectedly one beautiful summer morning. The air was warm and dry and the sun shone brightly. It looked like it would be another long, hot summer day in Texas. There was a gentle wind, just enough to help a person cool down, but not enough to kick up the dust and dirt so prevalent in this area of the country. It was a day that held the promise of long lazy evenings sipping iced tea or lemonade and of gentle conversations murmured softly in the warm twilight air after the heat of the afternoon.

Although I already had a life coaching certification, I was still working my normal eight to five job as a vocational rehabilitation counselor and doing lessons at our therapeutic riding center on the weekends. I had enrolled in a new certification program, the Touched by a Horse Equine Gestalt Coaching

Method, and was still six months away from graduation. I had practiced the method on my fellow students, read all the required books, and attended all the classes. And while I had facilitated some team-building workshops at my barn, I hadn't yet had the opportunity to do any real one-on-one coaching using my horses as partners in personal work. I wasn't even sure which of my horses would be interested in doing the work. Horses are a lot like humans in that respect. They don't all enjoy every type of work we sometimes ask them to do. They each have their own unique talents, abilities, interests, and preferences. At that point, I could only hope one or all of them would agree to work with me when the time came to have a client in the arena.

It was early and the heat of the day hadn't settled in yet. I was standing outside my office building enjoying the warmth of the sun and talking to a coworker about some issues she was having. We often took a few minutes throughout the day to take a short break to chat outside and enjoy the weather. We had talked about some of her issues before and I had given her some tools to work with. This morning was no different. As we stood talking, she seemed uneasy and worried. I could sense that she was struggling with some inner demons and was reluctant to talk about them. She'd had many physical problems lately and had missed a lot of work.

During the course of our conversation I asked her a simple question: "What's your point of view about your body?" She appeared to be frustrated by the question.

"I don't know," she replied. "Don't ask me any questions today. I don't want to think about it."

I told her to give it some thought when she was ready and we went back inside the building. I didn't think any more about it and returned to my office.

A few minutes later, before I could get started on the paperwork on my desk, she walked in, very upset and crying. She looked at me and said simply, "What if I blame myself?"

"Blame yourself for what?" I asked.

"Everything," she replied.

She said my question had brought up some things she had spent a lifetime trying not to think about. She believed everything that had happened might have been her fault, that she might have brought it all on herself. In the few minutes since we had come back inside, she had moved almost instantaneously into what psychologists call a shame spiral.

Recognizing what was happening, I knew it was necessary to deal with this immediately. I told her to sit down and closed the door to my office. She was distraught and couldn't stop crying. I asked her to tell me what she was feeling in that moment. She said that she was not comfortable discussing her issues in the office. Because she was familiar with my love of and work with the horses and what I was doing in the certification program, she asked if we could move this discussion to the barn. She said she felt the horses could really help her and she would be more at ease away from our coworkers. We agreed to meet there after she went home to put on more appropriate clothes. I let our supervisor know we would be leaving. Because I always carry barn clothes in my truck, I headed straight out to get things ready for our session.

All the way to the barn, I found myself wondering if I could really do this. Would I remember all I'd been taught and be able to help? And how would the horses react? After all, they hadn't done this work before either. Which horse should I ask? Would they understand what I needed them to do? Would they be willing to partner with me? I realized I didn't have a round pen set up. I also considered the fact that it was going to be so hot today and we would need to work outside. What if I made things worse or the horses wouldn't work with me? I didn't have a horse handler.

On and on it went. A million questions and thoughts buzzed around in my head like little gnats. I could feel myself becoming anxious and doubting my abilities to handle the situation. But then I remembered the most important thing I'd been taught in the certification program: trust your horses, trust yourself, and trust the process. Okay, I thought, I can do that. I repeated it to myself, over and over again. It became my mantra as I drove down the highway and turned off on the road that led to the barn.

When I arrived, I parked in the shade and stepped out of my truck. I stood for a minute, just quieting myself and breathing deeply. It was so silent and still. I was aware of birds singing somewhere in the back pasture and of a few bees buzzing near a small tree. The horses were milling about the paddock area, enjoying the early morning coolness. The aroma of fresh plowed earth, horses, and hay filled me with a sense of peace. I focused my attention on the ground beneath my feet and the warm air caressing my skin. I noticed the way the sun left shadows on the ground, and I watched the little motes of dust still floating gently in the air from my drive onto the property. I took another deep breath, gathered my courage, and walked to the gate.

The horses stood looking at me expectantly. They were not sure why I was there at this time of the morning. Every head was turned toward me, every eye watching me closely. I could sense their curiosity and found myself thinking how very lucky and grateful I was to have such magnificent creatures in my life.

My horses are older gents, all retired from their days of roping, riding, and ranching. They came to be here because they could no longer perform as they did when they were younger. Some had been injured and retired, others had boys and girls who had outgrown them and gone off to other lives in the city. They would spend the last years of their lives at this facility working as therapy horses for children with disabilities—hopefully, with me in the coaching process. When they could no longer work, they would be pastured and taken care of. I loved them deeply. Not seeing any children or noticing the usual routine of getting ready for lessons, they were curious and waited patiently to see what would happen next.

I greeted the herd and explained that I had someone coming who needed their help. I asked if anyone would be willing to partner with me to do this work, then waited quietly to see what would happen. Only a heartbeat later, sweet Danny, with his big liquid brown eyes, stepped up to the gate and nuzzled me through the pipe and cable that made up our fence. We stood quietly together for a moment. I scratched his neck, thanked him for volunteering, told him I knew he would be perfect for the job, and then stepped through the gate. He followed me into the arena and waited to see what I would do.

My friend arrived as I was setting up some chairs in the shade of the tack room. Danny noticed her first. I saw his head lift and his ears move forward. He turned away from me toward the drive and looked intently at the woman approaching. I had been so lost in my own thoughts that I didn't hear her drive up. She was still visibly upset, but had a determined stride as she moved across the drive. Danny immediately went to the gate and waited for her. When she entered, he walked up to her, and it was quite clear he knew exactly what she needed. While he was looking into her eyes, they made a connection— a bond if you will. They stood together for a moment and he gently placed his head on her shoulder telling her silently that she was safe and would be well cared for. She told me later that at that moment, for the first time in her life, she was able to recognize, feel, and begin to process the demons that had led her to where she was.

Not wanting to break the spell, I stood quietly for a minute before joining them at the gate. We all moved toward the arena together. Danny was completely at liberty, without halter or rope. He walked by her side as the other horses watched but didn't try to interfere or join us.

When we entered the arena, I closed the gate and offered her one of the chairs I had just placed there. I asked her to take a deep breath and just sit quietly for a moment. I reminded her (and myself, as well) that there was no other time or place, only now, and that she was safe. I could feel her apprehension and anxiety.

After a few minutes, she began to speak. Danny stood nearby listening to everything. The other horses stood quietly watching from the other side of the fence. I could sense their energy, their strength, and their support. I thanked them silently for holding space for us.

Quite suddenly, as we moved deeper into the session, Big walked to the arena gate and asked to be let in. This was very unusual and surprising, which was why it caught my attention. Although he was still and quiet, his message was clear. "I need to be in there with you. Let me in! Let me in!"

I was concerned since I already had Danny in the arena with us, but Big was so insistent that I finally asked my friend if she would be comfortable if he joined us.

"Please bring him in," she said.

So I did. I admit, at this point I had no idea what would happen, and I found myself thinking over and over again to trust the horses, trust the process.

We continued our session with both horses watching and listening to everything, but remaining polite and patient. A few minutes later, they both turned and walked away. Danny moved to the back pasture fence as if watching something interesting and Big walked to the water tank, although he didn't drink.

My friend was surprised at their sudden departure and wanted to know why they left. She seemed bereft that they would leave when she needed them so much. I ask her why she thought they left. She looked from me to them with a slightly bewildered expression before saying, "Because I'm trying to gloss over the issue and not being truthful."

I agreed. My feeling was she was not being authentic and the horses had lost interest. I reminded her that horses live completely in the moment and are not interested in us if we are not being authentic and living in the here and now. They will always call us out, one way or another. Although I had told her this before, for the first time, she seemed to understand. I asked her to take a deep breath and settle back down into her body. We then resumed our session.

As she became calmer and spoke from her heart, both horses moved back close to us and waited to see what would happen next. Big moved behind her and stood just a few feet away. She told me she could feel his strength. For the first time in her entire life she had the support she had always yearned for and had never received. She said that Big was her "rock" and he made her feel safe enough to continue the work.

After trying one or two different experiments, I could sense she was not feeling comfortable doing the work and was not fully immersing herself in the process. I no longer doubted her authenticity. Danny and Big had not only returned to us, but were paying rapt attention to everything that was happening.

At that moment, I had an epiphany of sorts and felt I knew exactly what she needed to help her through her issues. Her resistance thus far was mostly because some of the experiments we had attempted made her feel self-conscious and awkward. The beauty of the gestalt method of coaching is in the experience of following the energy and being able to change course in the middle of the process. It is in allowing yourself to utilize the tools you've learned in multiple ways and not having only one means to an end. It allows the client to attempt different modalities and pieces of work and immediately discard what's not working while moving into something more helpful. It is energy flow in its truest form. Gestalt is a dance between the coach and the client that moves always toward resolution of an issue. When the horses are included, the dance becomes magical and takes on a life of its own.

Danny had moved close to Big as we worked. Neither horse had offered any feedback at this point other than when they had briefly walked away. They stood side by side, silently watching and supporting my friend in her struggle with herself. I asked her to walk over to them and explained to her that I wanted her to go from one to the other and talk to them as if she were talking to the person who had caused her so much pain and conflict. I told her to look them in the eye and express what she was feeling about the issue at hand. I encouraged her to feel into her grief and sadness. I started the sentences for her and allowed her to finish them in any way she felt she needed.

As she moved from one horse to the other, I could see the tension in her body dissipate. The horses stood quietly, never moving a muscle as they listened with full attention to everything she said. They received her statements without judgment. She told them many things that had been left unsaid for years, speaking from her heart. She poured out all her feelings and left them there in the dirt of the arena, at the horses' feet. When she was done, she gave both horses big hugs, basking in their strength and energy. This in itself was remarkable because Big is often slightly head-shy and tends to lift his head up and out of the way when someone reaches up to touch him or halter him. On this day, however, he never moved or flinched. Both horses gently wrapped her in loving embraces.

We returned to our seats, and as we processed what had just happened, my friend pulled tissues from the box I had placed on the mounting step next to her chair. Danny, being ever vigilant, walked over and began to pull tissues from the box and drop them at her feet, although I noticed he considered eating one or two. He can be a real clown sometimes, but this was such a sweet and thoughtful act. It was as if he were saying "It's okay. Dry your tears. That wasn't really so bad, was it?" We laughed at his gesture and thanked him for his concern and kindness.

She told me she had never experienced this type of therapy and explained that the connection she felt with Danny made going through the process less painful. She said that Big made her feel safe enough to say the things she had been afraid to say for so many years. She also said that although she had gone to counseling in the past and had tried other means of dealing with her issues, nothing had ever helped her as much as her short time with us at the barn. She suddenly felt as if a big weight had been dropped from her shoulders. She would now be able to move forward into healing her life.

As we chatted, Danny started to leach. Over and over again he yawned, releasing the energy he had so willingly removed from her. She was alarmed until I explained why he was exhibiting what to her seemed such strange behavior. Then she began to cry again. This time, however, it was tears of gratitude.

It was such an amazing and humbling experience for me to have been a part of helping my friend move toward healing and to see the horses so generous and willing to step up and do what they do so naturally when we allow it. I think we often forget how big their hearts are and how willing their spirits are.

Although it's been many months since that warm summer day, my friend continues to tell me frequently how her experience with the horses changed her life. She tells me how she has learned to respond to situations rather than react. She tells me she feels calmer and doesn't worry about every little thing, as was her habit before her session with the horses. She understands that her work is not yet done and says she looks forward to the day when she gathers enough courage to look at the issues still remaining. She expresses her desire to experience again that strong connection and healing energy with the horses.

We both learned a lot that day, my friend and I. She began the beautiful process of healing years of disease and dysfunction in her life. With the help of the horses, she has been able to make positive changes and move forward with less anxiety, fear, and confusion. She often tells me she is frustrated because she is unable to find the words to express how profound the experience was.

And the horses, well, they just did what they always do. They offered support, love, energy, and assistance to us humans—who often mistakenly believe we are the superior beings on this planet. They did so without judgment, blame, or criticism. They held us in their loving energy and supported us in the process, helping us both come to new understandings about ourselves.

For me, it was a time of stepping into my truth. It was a time of learning to trust myself, my horses, and the process. It was a time of fully knowing that I am doing what I was sent here to do. It was an understanding that if I follow the energy and my intuition, and trust the process, all will be well.

Yes, it was a beautiful and unexpected experience that warm summer day. My friend, in all her pain, unknowingly gave me the most beautiful gift, the gift of trust.

Margo Green is the founder and CEO of Galloping to Greatness and cofounder and assistant director at Hold Your Horses Therapeutic Riding Center. She has a degree in psychology and more than twenty-five years' experience working with people with disabilities and the people who care for them. She also has over thirty years' experience in energy work. Through her company, Galloping to Greatness, Margo provides individual life coaching as well as group workshops. She brings a unique and creative approach to the area of coaching by partnering with her equine companions.

Margo Green
www.gallopingtogreatness.com

Growing into My Boots

Marnie Sears Branch

When I was a kid I used to love the catalogs that came in the mail from L.L. Bean. I loved all of the happy, smiling couples in beautiful wintery locations, and in the summer, the same healthy, tanned couples by the water. My favorite page was the one with all the boots. They were waterproof, sturdy, and hand stitched. I always wondered what kind of life I would have to create for myself in order to need boots like that. They looked like quality boots, something you would buy if you had a life that really required performance footwear. I had no such life.

After I divorced in my late thirties I started volunteering at Freedom Ride, a therapeutic riding facility in Orlando,

Florida. I was simultaneously completing a fifteen-month course to learn life coaching. I wanted to take my bad divorce experience and create something good out of it, something I might be able to use to help others. I loved coaching and hearing the relief in someone's voice after an insight that changed their way of thinking for good. After I graduated, I wanted to enhance my education somehow and was looking around for another program, but I just wasn't sure what I wanted to try next.

Freedom Ride and I were a good match. It was hard for me to get out there every week, but I found that the time there made a difference in how I felt the rest of the week. While I was there I had no unpleasant thoughts about my ex-husband. I wasn't disturbed by anything; I was never tense. I was learning so much about the animals, and I soon realized that they brought a very particular kind of peace to my life. Even if I was shoveling stables and wading through wood chips and horse nuggets, I was still deliriously happy when I was there. I didn't have to wear makeup. I didn't have to iron my tee shirts since I was going to leave filthy anyway. Plus, all the volunteers had the coolest boots. But while I envied them from afar, I still didn't find it necessary to buy them. I wasn't an equestrian. I didn't really work with horses, even though it had been a dream of mine for years to ride and learn to care for them. I decided to wait before I bought boots, but I wasn't sure what I was waiting for.

I had been volunteering for about three months when I woke up one morning and found a heavy gray sky and pouring rain. I dressed in my volunteer tee shirt and denim shorts and put on my old Converse sneakers. I tossed a raincoat and a bandana in the car and drove through the rain to the stable. The downpour stopped on the way there, but I knew we were in for a day of rain and it wasn't just a quick shower. The rain was threatening to come down again at any moment.

The property was so green it hurt to look at it in the wet mist. I joined the other volunteers and walked the eight resident horses to pasture before I went to go muck stables. It was about thirty minutes later, when I went to dump my wheelbarrow on the manure pile, that I realized I had created a space for boots in my life. As I stood there struggling to tip out all the manure and urine-soaked woodchips, I felt something cold on my feet. I looked down and found myself standing in a murky brown puddle of manure and dirty runoff from the pile. My beige sneakers were now brown, and it had soaked through my socks. I was horrified. I squelched my way through the morning and took the shoes off before I got into my SUV to leave.

After I ordered my waterproof boots online, I started doing research on coaching with animals. I had the idea of doing retreats that would include riding, but even that seemed like a bad idea since I wasn't an expert horsewoman. I felt I needed direction, and I had no idea how to tie it into divorce recovery or how to insure myself for that kind of liability. I eventually found a website for Touched by a Horse, whose owner, Melisa Pearce, had developed a method of coaching with the horses, themselves. According to the site, I didn't need my own horses and I didn't have to be an expert rider or trainer. I didn't have to live on a ranch. I didn't have to be a coach, but I was. I thought it might be a good fit and proceeded to gather information, despite the fact that it sounded fairly New Age and I wasn't sure about that aspect of the program.

By the time my boots arrived on my doorstep two weeks later, I had registered for an informational call and was due to receive a package in the mail that explained the program in detail. That night, my boyfriend came over to find me ecstatically trying on my boots while wearing my pajamas. We had planned to stay in and watch movies, but I was clomping happily around my little apartment in my blue boots, realizing that I had made one small dream come true. Jason was laughing at me, but I didn't care. I insisted that he take my picture in them.

In January, Jason and I moved in together and I started the Touched by a Horse program. It was an odd adjustment period. I had just taken two leaps of faith at once, but after a while we settled into what turned out to be a pretty good life. Spring came. I was attending my classes by phone every week, talking to my program coach every two weeks, and reading a lot of material on horses, natural horsemanship, and communication with animals. In my classes I was learning about birth order, chakras, deepening interactions with people, coaching methods, and marketing. Melisa was kind and friendly, but also very serious about her work, which I loved and respected. I knew that I had done the right thing for myself.

But I still wished my rapport with the horses at Freedom Ride was better. I felt bullied by them. When I got to the gate in the mornings to put them in the pasture, they put their big, broad faces squarely against my back and pushed me, trying to get me to go faster. I was shoved into gates, squished into walls and stable doors, and one particularly fresh horse nibbled on me for an entire thirty minute lesson while I was horse handling. In their minds I was nothing more than a skinny obstacle.

138

But then I saw what kind of power they were truly capable of and fear crept into my thoughts. Ivan, the resident Arabian mix, was being turned into the pasture one day, and as the volunteer unclipped the buckle on his halter, he bolted, hooves thundering as he raced away from her. The volunteer's face registered fear, and I was grateful the be on the other side of the fence. I had no idea that you could actually feel their gallop in your chest like a drumbeat. It took my breath away, and I was afraid of Ivan for months after that incident.

Eight months after I started Touched by a Horse, I went to my first CORE weekend training. I wrapped my boots in a plastic bag and tossed them into my luggage. They were too filthy to take otherwise. I was nervous about the travel, nervous about the intense work, and nervous about speaking in front of everyone. What if I didn't like it? What if I didn't like my classmates? What if I had just wasted a lot of money on tuition for something I didn't really understand? I understood the curriculum easily, but I was worried about the hands-on work and how the horses would treat me.

I sat in the circle of women that night for the first time and looked closely at all of them. They were all beautiful, strong women who looked like they could take on anything. Their denim-clad legs were stretched into the center of the circle as they sat back in their chairs, and I noted a lot of boots. Was it time for me to buy another pair? Did I look like these women? Was I one of them?

The minute they started talking about what they were feeling I knew that the answer was yes. There was a lot of nervousness present, a lot of love, self-discovery, and joy in companionship. I was in the right place.

My stomach was in knots for the first two days. I would see Melisa looking speculatively at us and believed she could tell what thoughts were in our minds and what they were presenting as in our bodies. I was anxious about the deep process work to come and about taking my turn to try it. I had seen small pieces of work over the last few days that had been beautiful representations of what the horses could do with a human partner. Now I wanted to know what it felt like to be in the arena with them doing the work.

On the third morning I got my chance to see how it felt as I sat in the empty chair in front of Melisa and looked into her brown eyes. She smiled at me and kept looking directly into my eyes. I took a deep breath; she took one too.

"So, what can I do for you today, Marnie?" she asked, as though we were in a shop and I was about to ask for something on a high shelf.

"I'm here to let go of my ex-husband. I feel I've done a lot of the work already, but there's still something left, one aspect that I can't get rid of." I reached for my heart, placing my hand there like I always did when I talked about something that hurt me or when I witnessed pain in others. It was a physical presence inside my chest, and it hurt. I was wearing a microphone so the students could hear me and my voice was loud in the barn. I consciously lowered it and kept going, even though my voice shook.

She nodded and waited. I told her what I was struggling with—mainly the fact that I had never had any closure because my ex-husband refused to speak to me. I needed to slam the door shut on my pain for good. Still, I felt horrible about everything, and I was so angry.

I finished quickly, not wanting to dwell on any one part of it and not wanting to tell the story again. I had a problem with dumping this last bit of anger. In my mind, I had told her all she needed to know, and if it wasn't enough, I trusted that she would ask me for more information.

She didn't ask for anything else. She just had me go into the round pen with a large black mare named Proud Mary. Proud Mary was in foal, getting a bit thick around the middle, and had chronic gas. She had actually been my favorite horse all weekend, despite her loud and frequent gastric disturbances.

Melisa asked me to circle the pen and talk about being single instead of in a relationship. I thought for a moment while I looked at my feet in my blue boots, then I heard Mary begin to follow me with interest. I recalled one particular morning when I had been living in my first apartment as a single woman. It had been a cold morning for central Florida and I had put an old quilt on my bed the night before. I had windows on either side of my bed and it was the bright sunlight that woke me up that morning. When I opened my eyes, the first thing I saw were the soft colors of the quilt and my sweet calico cat, Cricket, curled up next to my hip, purring loudly in a patch of white light. She opened her eyes and we looked at each other for a moment as her purr got louder. The room was chilly and the sunlight was beautiful and welcome. Cricket's bright coat had glowed and I had been suddenly and intensely happy. I voiced this memory to Melisa. Both Mary and the group began to follow me closely. Melisa said that it meant I was in alignment with my true feelings and asked me to go to the center of the pen and stand still.

I did this and she asked me how I would feel about declaring myself single and celibate for a while in order to know what my heart truly wanted. I thought about it a moment and closed my eyes to be in tune with what I was feeling. My body was still shaking, but I couldn't tell if I was cold or nervous.

"It would be a relief," I finally said. And then I felt a wall of heat approach me from my right side. I opened my eyes as Mary's big body brushed mine. She walked so close to me that she was nearly forcing me to step back and the heat from her felt very strong. I was startled by the experience. She stopped moving when our bellies were pressed together. Hers was full of possibility—new life and growth. Mine was literally empty. I'd barely been able to eat that morning and had barely been able to eat for my whole marriage. I never felt stable, I could never fully relax into it. I was constantly on the deck of a rocking ship and I was always sick. I realized how it had manifested as me punishing myself for all the things he had blamed me for. Sadly, I had believed him enough to deny myself better health and well-being.

Mary was breathing gently and just standing there, offering me her warmth and peace. I stood perfectly still, afraid to move and ruin the moment. The contact felt so comforting, right where I needed it. Mary seemed to pulse with heat and I asked Melisa if I could place my hands on her. She said yes, and I gently placed my palms on her beautiful dark back. I still wasn't sure what was happening, but Melisa said she was clearing my chakras.

Suddenly it was over. Mary walked away. Melisa said I was all done and she opened the gate for me to step out of the round pen. She was smiling as I passed by her.

My legs and hands were shaking violently and I didn't think they would ever stop. I went straight to the conference room that we used for meals and breaks and stood there, trying to figure out what I needed to do for myself in that moment. One of the women walked in and put her arms around me.

"You were great," she said, smiling at me. "We've had similar experiences. I really identified with what you said."

I smiled and thanked her. Then I realized that I was hungry—seriously, ravenously hungry. I got a snack and some water and went back out with the group. Mary had her head down in the round pen, sniffing the wood chips. You would never know that she was a working girl with a special skill set and not just a pregnant mare.

I ate twice on the flights home. I called Jason before the last flight and told him I needed to eat and that I hoped we could stop on the way home. He seemed confused, but acknowledged my request. He acknowledged it again the next day when I asked him to cook eggs and bacon for breakfast and chicken and rice for dinner. A week later he was staring at me as I sat in front of our coffee table with an entire feast of Chinese food spread around me from the local takeout. I was slurping down noodles and hot chicken soup when I noticed his expression and his silence. His fork was poised in midair and he was looking at me with a sense of wonder.

"What happened?" he asked.

"What do you mean?" I said around a mouthful of lo mein.

"To you. Out there . . . in Virginia. Did they feed you guys? Did they allow you to eat?"

I nodded yes. The food had been wonderful, home cooked by one of the hosts and delivered to us daily. I told him this.

"I've never seen you eat like this. It's been a whole week. I can't tell if I'm proud or scared."

"I feel like I shut the door on my marriage," I said after hesitating a moment. "I punished myself the whole time I was married by not eating and not taking care of my needs. He always came first, and I denied myself so many things because I believed all the awful things he said about me and to me. I want to make up for it. I want to feel good again. I don't know how else to explain it except to say that the horse had something to do with it. I walked away and I felt clear, like something I had been carrying was gone."

He nodded and listened, but then smiled as I resumed eating. He was smiling a month later when my jeans started to get tight. He was still smiling and also laughing another month after that when I spent five hundred dollars buying all new pants that would actually fit me. It was three months before I attended the next CORE and I had gained fifteen pounds in that time. At the time of my divorce, I was a size zero on a five-foot-ten frame, and I was truly ill. I felt horrible and had no energy. Now I was a size six with hips, and I loved the way I looked and felt. I had never been able to gain weight. Now I had and I felt like a normal human being. I wasn't afraid to have bare arms in pictures because they no longer looked like sticks. I wore skirts and jeans with a good fit. I was comfortable in my own skin.

It had paid off in other ways too. I wasn't close to fainting after cleaning stables. I felt robust and healthy and listened to my body when I needed something. I ate a wider variety of food and tried new things. I was enjoying my life in a manner that I had never before experienced, and I wasn't as afraid of things as I had been.

I had believed that the work I did that day when I stepped into the pen with Mary would be all about my husband and our abusive marriage. It felt good to say what I needed to say and acknowledge that I needed help letting go. Once I truly did get closure with that, he was much less present in my thoughts and I was able to stop myself from thinking about him when he did pop up. Thinking about him no longer gave me physical pain or sensations of sweating or shaking. He was insignificant now, and I was intensely grateful for the peace that brought me.

What I had not expected was to have the largest part of my realization be about how I had neglected to care for myself during those years with him. I knew I would place myself in high regard now. I could count on that; I could count on myself. I would take care of myself, and I was worthy of being cared for.

When I got home I bought another pair of boots to acknowledge my growth and change. They were blue willies—expensive since my tastes ran in that direction when it came to footwear for the stable—and I loved them. They were celebration boots, boots that I could walk through anything in. I had walked through so much already and at times simply ducked my head and ran. But I knew what I was doing on some level and I knew it would all become clear.

I can't wait to start doing this work with my own clients. I want to see how it affects others. And I want to honor them when they laugh, cry, or simply stand in silence with the horses and feel the power of their tremendous energy.

When I went back to Freedom Ride I took some new skills with me. One of the women at the CORE had worked with me on teaching a horse to walk and stop using my intention and visual cues. When I got home I tried it on the Freedom Ride horses. I haven't said, "Whoa," or "Walk on" since she trained me. I don't need to talk at all and it feels like a miracle every time a horse respectfully stops next to my shoulder without a word passing between us. I am no longer bullied. I have learned to let them come to me on their terms and to be as gentle and respectful with them as possible. I look to myself first when I see them make mistakes. My third CORE is in two weeks and I am eyeing my first pair of cowboy boots. Just a starter pair. The really nice ones will be when I graduate from this program. I will have earned them.

Marnie Bench is a life coach in Orlando, Florida, specializing in divorce recovery for women. She began her training with Coach U and continued from there to Touched by a Horse, where she is pursuing certification as an Equine Gestalt Coach. Marnie began her training with horses as a volunteer with Freedom Ride of Central Florida and now volunteers with the Equine Angels Foundation in Orlando. She writes short fiction and poetry, and she maintains a blog on divorce recovery and empowerment for women. Her passion is seeing women thrive and recognize their worth after leaving relationships that don't serve their highest good. She still buys boots to celebrate milestones in her work and her life!

Marnie Bench
www.marniebenchcoaching.net
Marnie.bench@gmail.com

My Awakening

Michelle Griffith

The significance of the number forty among spiritual scholars of all dimensions is not new. This time period can be referenced as days, months, or years. It can be a period of testing, trial, or probation ending with a period of restoration, revival, or renewal. For me, it has been a tale of forty years in wait of spiritual awakening to follow my soul's path in this life.

Horses have been a part of my life since the moment I was born. For some people horses are an addiction. I am one of those people, but really couldn't put my finger on why until I started this journey as an Equine Gestalt Coach. Horses are my connection to divine love, truth, and being. I feel better in their presence and long for contact with them when I have to be away.

As a child growing up in a super conservative rural environment, I didn't even know that there were people who practiced spirituality outside of Christian denominations, let alone anyone who would find a spiritual connection with energy—and especially energy from animal beings.

My first experience with horses who spoke to me came at about age five. My mother's family had horses and I don't ever recall a Sunday get-together when we didn't go out and ride or take a trip into town with the pony cart. My dad was the type of guy who tended to gamble, so his horses were heavy and work oriented. They were for competition, pulling of sleds weighted down by cinder blocks. I don't remember all their names. I think Doc and Duke were full-size Belgians, but the ones who touched me were Thunder and Lightning.

In my mind, Thunder and Lightning were *huge*, but they were just an average team of pulling ponies. They were beautiful in my eyes with reddish-blonde coats and beautiful blonde manes and tails. They had big fancy shoes called pulling cleats that helped them to gain traction when it was time to pull, but we had to be very careful because if you got stepped on, it could mean some serious damage or possibly the loss of some toes! I wasn't ever scared of them. I remember how they always put their big soft noses to my head and blew my hair. I loved that.

My biggest thrill came the day when we were at a pulling contest and my dad entered me into the powder-puff class, much to my mom's dismay. The classification was for kids ten and under, and while I was five, most of the other kids were much closer to the age of ten. I got to pick which horse I wanted to use and I immediately said, "Thunder."

Mom threw a fit. She wanted me to go out there with one of the big horses that was gentle and trustworthy. She was very upset that Dad would send me out there with the one horse in the lineup that was genuinely unpredictable. He was very powerful for his size and radiated the true wild horse roots of fight-or-flight attitude.

Thunder told me that he could do it without me, but we would have fun out there together. This was a horse who whispered directly into my brain with his warm breath as he gently puffed the hair on top of my head. I had the distinct awareness that he wanted to share the joy of his work with me rather than the stress of competition like he had when Dad's hands were on the reins.

The horses got prancy and on the muscle whenever they stepped on deck to pull and Thunder gave the best show of this. Often a handful for my dad, he was undefeated and had an attitude to match. He was like a keg of dynamite waiting to ignite, and that was the thing that attracted me to him. He was beautiful and embodied pure horsepower. When I walked out there to the on deck area, Thunder was just a little playful. He radiated fun and play, as if he were about to take me over the river and through the woods to Grandmother's house.

The hitch pin clanked and Thunder catapulted forward with great force to pull the load. After we crossed the finish line, we unhooked the hitch and he dropped his muzzle right on my head with a big snort of horse laughter. That simple snort of air filled me with pure joy. The purity of that moment filled me with a peaceful joy that only a five-year-old can fully experience because at five, we are still able to be present in the moment and receive the gift of joy.

What I didn't realize until forty years later was that the gift Thunder gave me in that moment was love and joy in the purest form. It filled the cave of my heart with energy that would hold me all through the journey of my life. Knowledge of being in the moment, experiencing it fully and finding the joy in it, was now a part of me. That snort of breath into my crown chakra from a sweet little crazy horse named Thunder was a gift that that would serve me well in my life's journey.

Throughout my life, horses have held me up, challenged me, and provided healing and therapy for stresses and hurts, always filling me with love and light when I needed it most. They have blessed me with lessons direct from Source, exactly at the moment when I was present and able to hear the whispers.

I got to see the best and the worst of the horse/human condition on the road for ten years as a salesperson in the horse industry. I saw horses abused and overworked, spurred in the sides to the point of scarring on their skin, jerked in the face until their lips were bleeding. I saw giant raw strips of flesh and scars across noses from "training aids." I saw tails lengthened, broken, propped, deadened, abscessed, and unable to function to swat flies, all in the name of fashion.

There were contraptions and special shoes to encourage higher hock and knee action, ginger put into the rectum to have the horse hold their tail high, whipping to cause "alertness" for the show ring, and, worst of all, horses neglected and starving. I saw hooves curling up and horses unable to walk. Some foundered and others were just too weak to stand. How was it that these creatures continued to live with humans instead of jumping the fence and running away? I could not understand it.

I saw the best of conditions too: horses with padded floors in stalls and scheduled veterinary and farrier support; horses who received regular massages, acupuncture, and Reiki treatments; horses who got groomed twice a day; and horses who lived in barns with clean air exchangers, temperature control, and automatic watering stations. And probably the horses who were happiest of all were those who had really nice turnout pastures that were fertilized, rotated, clipped, and maintained with a full staff of ranch hands. I met horses who made trainers famous and some who starred in movies.

Along this path I encountered the first horse outside of those on my family farm who would become my partner and whisper to my heart. He was a beautiful Arabian gelding whose name, Wispring, was a combined form of his sire, Wisdom, and his dam, Springtime. There was a lot of talk about this little horse's pedigree and show success, which was impressive, but those things held no meaning for me. This horse was aware of people in a way that has made Arabians legends.

I didn't even have a place to keep a horse, but I knew that I had to find a way to have this horse in my presence. There were things he wanted to teach me. Some very good friends had an open stall and allowed me to keep Wispring there in exchange for help with feeding and cleaning stalls. He provided me brush therapy like only an Arabian could do. His stunning beauty made me grateful for the gift of a horse in my world and the power of his heart connected me back to the earth and refocused my attention on my life's journey. My husband and I eventually settled on a nice five acre spot and built a barn.

As I continued on in the horse business, one particular barn that served people as a therapy center inspired me to follow my urge to teach. Whether physical, mental, or emotional "deficits" had been identified, all the human souls who found a way to that barn responded in the same way. They were "better" in the presences of horses. It was like magic and it worked every time.

Many times prior to visiting the therapy barn, I felt the calling to teach. "Teach" meant public school setting to me. I had wanted to be a teacher in college and considered changing my major to education. But I wondered how being a teacher would keep me in close contact with horses, so I finished my degree in agriculture. I was trained in animal science and journalism. I hoped to stay close to the industry and write for a trade publication.

The urge to teach landed me in the midst of 4-H as a county agent. It was a lot more like experiential learning than teaching, and it filled me up in a tangible way. The experience gave me an opportunity to witness so much learning in the presence of and care for animals.

Eventually, I finished my master's degree in education. I was especially attracted to students with disabilities. I always found myself thinking of that therapy barn and how much joy was experienced there with the horses. I spent my time in graduate school subbing for experience in all types of classes, with teachers and students who had a wide variety of gifts and skill sets. What I learned was that students with disabilities are often purest of heart.

In 2011, I attended the Ohio Equine Affaire. The friend that I had planned to meet there was running behind schedule, so I had some extra time to take in a presentation. I looked at the schedule and in five minutes there was an interesting offering by Melisa Pearce about healing and chakras in horses. It had to do with recognizing blocked energy and the benefits of correcting the energy flow. I thought the presentation would be about how you can pick up on what is physically happening with your horse by looking at his energy. It was some of that, but more about how horses sense, experience, channel, and communicate energy, as well as how horses are gifts of spirit who can help humans heal at the energetic and soul level.

I couldn't stop thinking about how horses receive and experience human energy. Horses are willing partners with any person who is open to receive and participate in their own healing experience. I remembered that day of pure joy with Thunder. I thought back over the ten years I had spent in the horse industry in and out of a multitude of different barns— all full of horses with jobs to do and all radiating different types and levels of energy. I thought of how that energy ranged from purest love to darkness and pain.

I checked into this idea of healing with horses and ended up pursuing the Equine Gestalt Coaching Method with Melisa Pearce. At the first intensive training session called CORE, I showed up at Melisa's place in Colorado (just two weeks after signing up for the program) and could not stop crying. All through the weekend, as the horses worked individually with other students, I was in awe of their huge hearts and sensitivity to the human condition. And I was extremely aware of how much the horses were tuned in to me. And most importantly, I was aware of their ability to heal so many energetic anomalies in humans.

A beautiful mare named Tory had her moment to assist Melisa with another student and it was all I could do to hold it together. As the student worked on her awareness, Tory held space, moved energy, communicated with Melisa, and balanced the client's chakra energy. I had to leave the barn to compose myself. I was physically shaking in a way that I had never experienced. It wasn't fear, but it was shaking from the cellular level. I couldn't believe how this big healing energy was impacting me at the physical level, in addition to the emotional and spiritual levels.

Finally, when it was my opportunity to work, each of the seven horse spirits in the barn showed up front and center to volunteer to work with me. It was Shadow who stepped into the round pen. It has been said that he is just a plain brown horse. He is far from plain. He is big and powerful and his heart energy was the size of the mountains in view out the back door of the arena. He was present, in the moment. And he was there to meet me exactly where I was. He had no judgment and no agenda, he was just present in the purest form of presence. As I discovered the root of my tears, Shadow just waited patiently for me to unload my stuff so he could carry it away for me.

The pure love and joy breathed into my heart by Thunder on that day of the pulling contest when I was five years old could no longer be kept in the "shadow" of my "life." It was no accident that this beautiful bay horse named Shadow was fully present to ignite that beautiful gift of light—the ember in the cave of my heart delivered on the breath of Thunder.

My piece of work at that moment was to push through all the shadows of hurt and ugliness thrust upon horses that I had witnessed in my life. My apology to equus on behalf of humans was the key to igniting the ember in my heart. Shadow just stood there and took all the pain away. He actually walked away and gave a full body shake to get rid of the stuff he held on my behalf. Then he returned to me, licked my hands, and asked me to make a further agreement to become a light worker on behalf of horses, to give them a voice and make their place in the world one of value rather than one of serving as objects for the prestige or convenience for their humans.

My connection with Shadow was simply a *Namaste* experience.

"*Namaste*, dear Shadow. I honor the place in you where the entire universe resides. I honor the place in you of light, love, truth, peace, and wisdom." I honor and share this place of connection free from time and ego, deep from the heart where a union of spirits can blossom.

All throughout the EGCM apprentice training I observed horses working energetically with people and shifting their consciousness through the energy of their hearts. There are individual horses who can balance chakras, interpret energy for humans who struggle to verbalize what is on their mind, and—my personal favorites—those who are lie detectors.

During my CORE experiences, while attempting to assist another person on their journey, I discovered that horses not only have the energy and ability to support the client, but also have the capacity to ignite the light in my heart as if I were plugged into the energy of the sun. The horse partner holds my heart so I can stay focused as a life coach and grounded energetically to effectively hold space for the client working through their piece.

It is no accident that I am starting this journey as an Equine Gestalt Coach forty years after the breath of joy from Thunder that put an ember of God's love and light into the cave of my heart. I am on my soul's path in this life. The gifts of horses in my world are now clear to me. They fill me with spirit from Source. They are a pure conduit for presence and true love. Together with horses I am here to assist humans to discover true love from Source that feeds their soul. I am here to serve and work for the greater good and to be a voice for the healing power of horses.

Namaste.

Michelle Griffith has a Bachelor of Science in Agriculture from Ohio State University and a Master's in Education from Wright State University. She has held positions as a facilitator, trainer, coach, and teacher since 1990. Horses have always been a part of Michelle's life and she has found great comfort in brush therapy—having the opportunity to walk into the barn and recover some internal balance by making contact with her horses in a simple grooming session. She reconnected with horse healing modalities in response to becoming emotionally battered and bruised in an unhealthy work environment. A total commitment to success at any cost left her feeling anxious, irritable, and overwhelmed. Now Michelle spends most of her time working to establish her EGCM practice at Mane Rise Coaching. Other projects include work on a novel, teaching Hatha Yoga, and integrating tools and techniques from Ayurveda to assist people in a holistic approach to balance for mind, body, and spirit.

Michelle Griffith
Mane Rise Coaching
www.manerisecoaching.com

Wild Ponies of the Globe

Barbra Broxterman

As the evening globe passes over the prairie grass high,
And circles the sphere where the mountains honor the sky,
The wild ponies pound the ground, turning this great sphere
   beneath their feet,
While in syncopated motion the heart of the earth and their
   sprits meet.
Hooves drum out the ancestral rhythm in first two than a
   three part flight,
As globe and ponies dance with the sun, the moon, and the
   silent jewels of the night.

Gazing they stand alert, nostrils flared; inhaling all that was
   and is to be.
Bays, browns, palominos and grays, manes flowing, tails high
   and free.

Tapping out a grateful message to the sweet earth and pools
    of life they find,
Circling, beginning to end, bodies sway in parallel motion of
    space but no time,
Boldly they stride forward, necks like giant pendulums,
    moving the energy up and back into the ground.
Assuring the sphere's return season after season to replenish,
    renew and again go round.

To all the babies here and gone. . . .

Holding Space

Barbra Broxterman

Deep in the forest where trees stand proud and tall,
Surrounded by fragrant flowers and the eagles shrill call,
A whirl of time in continuum, a space forever new,
Tis held for a child's essence, created, sacred and true.

Thus I stand transfixed, next to a large, dark, handsome bay,
Smelling of sweat, manure, earth and fresh cut hay,
Aligning his torso next to mine, supporting back, our
    energies entwine,
My child, my child I whisper, please know you belong.

My grief is old, yet strong, from things said or done wrong,
Legs they shake, I forget to breath, there is release, my body
    heaves.
Long ago or was it yesterday, your light, your soul, passed
    away,
Leaving me sorrow locked, away, not shared; never put on
    display.

The gelding scans me up and down, his head then rests near
    the ground.
Ears twitch, eyes soft, he reads my sorrow, absorbs my pain.
No sound is spoke, no picture drawn, he speaks to my soul,
    rights my wrong.

In my mind's eye, a vision I see, it's not from me, but from the
    heart of he.

"We all have a purpose like the rain, this pain should not be
    held nor contained,
It is yours, it is mine, it is all of ours,
Part wind, part rain, part sky;
Part earth, it is radiant, not a burden and not a stain."

No matter how tiny, with lungs not formed
Or as a superb being, shouting to the wide open air,
I see you as the wild wind blowing the winter leaves,
And the mane of equus, flowing, cascading and running free.

This whirl of time and continuum is yours to know,
As days unmeasured your spirit unfolds,
A space bigger than the universe was created for you.
A grand love, where with the seasons, your spirit endures.

This quantum dimension was prepared, when you entered
    the fold,
You are part of and belong to all the promises' shared
    and untold.
Know love, feel my arms around you from afar,
As I surrender and embrace the truth that you are.

My eyes they open, my breath I feel,
The bay beside me, stands there still,
Then offers me one last gift of grace,
Complete acceptance of holding space.

Come light, come love, come hope, come grace, come
gratitude for you.
You are the whirl of time in continuum, a space forever new,
Which is held for your essence, created, sacred and true.

Barbra Broxterman is the owner of Wayfinding with Horses,
an agricultural engineer, a natural horse practitioner, a
breeder of Andalusian Horses (King of King Horses), and a
grass fed beef operator. Wayfinding with Horses is a personal
coaching business that positively assists and encourages those
searching to understand themselves better, explore new possibilities, make life changes, deal with losses, or develop their
own personal trail or path towards a more purposeful life.

Barbra Broxterman
wwww.wayfindingwithhorses.com

A Horse, a Coach, and a Beautiful Triad

Nancy Lee Gerson

One morning I had a private equine gestalt coaching session with my client Tamara. We began by sitting together and "pausing"—allowing the listening to go wide while staying connected to our bodies, our senses, and the present moments as they came to pass. My red roan horse, Saint, was already in the round pen just a few feet away. After a few minutes, I handed Tamara a deck of *Touched by a Horse Inspiration Cards*, and when she was ready, she pulled the "Mystical" card.

She immediately exclaimed, "Oh, this is perfect! Do you see that?" She read aloud the entire passage on her card, and as I listened, I considered the various props to collect and store for my coaching work. I asked Tamara if anything from the card particularly struck her. She looked it over and read a few sentences. "Surrender" and "release" were among the words she read.

What suddenly arose in my mind was an image of Tamara plucking out blossoms and petals from a plastic flower bouquet, tossing them down to the ground, and surrendering and releasing whatever was there to be surrendered or released.

I retrieved the bouquet and handed it to her. Briefly explaining the experiment, I directed her to walk around the outside of the round pen, completing either the sentence, "I surrender . . ." or "I release . . ." as she tossed the petals and blossoms along her circular journey.

I watched Tamara start to walk around, and I also kept an eye on Saint. It was so beautiful to witness Tamara's obvious earnestness and deliberateness while experimenting in this way. She was opting for silent speech. From where she first started out, she wasn't very near to where Saint was, on the inside of the round pen. But, eventually, she came to the panel that was very close to him. As this happened, Saint looked up from his grazing on the few bits of hay in evidence, and stood stock-still for the several seconds it took Tamara to toss down a flower and then resume her walking. Once she did so, Saint immediately started to walk along with her, stopping whenever she stopped and resuming his walk whenever she resumed hers.

At some point after this, Tamara came back over to the chairs and sat down. Before I could even ask her if she might like to go into the round pen with Saint now, she announced that she wanted to tell me about what had taken place. Naturally, I welcomed the prospect of hearing all about it.

She told me how perfect it was that I had given her the bouquet to carry. She described how the big, white flowers "represented the purity of my ancestors," and that she had honored them during her walk. And then she said, pointing to certain yellow buds, that they represented thorns and thorny things she had surrendered and released during the walk.

I was struck by the deep wisdom of a triad she had just named into existence: honor, surrender, release. I shared this with her, specifically acknowledging that it was her very own wisdom. We shared a few moments of wonderment at how this was yet another example of "threes" in her life. She has rescued three horses, their names all begin with the letter "S" (Symphony, Star, and Spirit), and so on.

Drawing in the air and space between us, I suggested to her that her triad physically looked like so:

This image resonated with Tamara in a very full way, but I didn't encourage a lot of talking around this. Instead, it was time for movement, action—specifically, interaction with my partner Saint. I asked her to join Saint inside the round pen. There was no need to ask her how comfortable she was being around horses, because I already knew she had horses of her own. Also, she had previously met my herd.

Before she had even arrived at the center and started to ground herself with my guiding words, Saint was approaching her—sweet, wise Saint. I suggested that Tamara start walking around the inside perimeter of the round pen, completing and repeating either "I surrender," or "I release," or whatever other formulation might arise for her during this new phase of the coaching session.

Again, she opted to walk in silence or, at least, I could not hear anything from her from where I was seated. As soon as she began to walk out towards the rails, Saint followed her and walked around with her the whole time, staying just off of her shoulder.

They traveled around in a full circle, and when the two of them returned to the center again, Saint stayed very close to Tamara, with his head nearly touching hers. They stayed like this for a while as I witnessed in silence. At some point, I asked Tamara if there was someone or something that had not yet been surrendered or released. If so, did she want to take advantage of the opportunity to finish that piece of unfinished business? I assured her that it was fine if there was nothing she felt was unfinished or if there was but she did not want to work with it further at this time.

She said yes, there was more and, yes, she did want to work on that as well. She had meandered away from the center slightly, so I had her move back into it. As she brought herself to stillness once again, Saint chose to place himself a few feet away from her, but facing her straight on. He stood there very still, very silent, and very clearly connected to his client. The directness of his stance and his glance were quite striking to me.

I picked up the bouquet that was now lying just outside the round pen gate and brought it inside to Tamara. I placed it at her feet, then repositioned it slightly so the white flowers were not touching the dirt. I looked up at her then, explaining that I had done this in remembrance that those blooms represented her ancestors. Her grin of appreciation was huge!

She started walking around the round pen. This time, Saint initially stayed put. However, as soon as Tamara had walked right behind him and cleared the far side of his rear end, Saint turned his whole body around and took a small step towards her.

But then he stopped walking and, instead, did these three things, in quick sequence: lifted his tail and passed gas; made some mouth and tongue "leeching" movements; and lowered his neck and head all the way to the ground. By this time, Tamara had walked past a few more panels and had her back to Saint.

I was so struck by these releases that I ventured to break into the silent flow, quietly calling out to Tamara. I felt compelled to share with her what had just taken place outside her field of vision. When she looked over at me, I saw her tear-filled eyes. I commented that she must be doing some powerful releasing and described what Saint had been up to—his stunning mirroring and reflecting back.

After that, I had Tamara return to the center with Saint, and in the tradition that I've created for all of my coaching events, I invited Tamara not only to thank Saint, but also to take as much time as she needed to tell him what qualities she saw in him. She did this silently and then came out of the round pen. Pausing outside the gate, she remarked, "Wow, I'm so exhausted." I escorted her over to the chairs, and we sat together for a minute before I handed her a bottle of water.

Before rising from her chair, Tamara picked up the card she had selected from the deck at the outset. She made a comment or two about how even the background color was symbolic for her. I smiled and told her that the card was hers to keep as a gift with which to remember the session.

Later in the day, I received a text message from her, asking me to remind her of one of the triad words (surrender.) It made me happy to know that hours later, the deep work she had done was still coursing through her mind and heart. Amen.

Up until July, 2010, **Nancy Gerson**, who is fluent in English and Spanish, was a practicing attorney in NYC with children, dogs, and cats, but no horses. Within four months of attending a women's horseback riding retreat outside of Estes Park,

Colorado, Nancy had relocated to Longmont, Colorado, giving up her law practice, rock and roll band, and proximity to friends and family. In the process, she gained a life with horses—specifically, Cherokee, the horse she rode on retreat, plus two more, Saint and Dalai Lama. Hers is a story of being moved by the heart, literally.

Nancy Gerson
Saddle Up Your Spirit: *Get Your Quest On!*
www.saddleupyourspirit.com

Rhiannon

Paula Karen

A Pronouncement delivered from the Fairy Eponalisa to Grace, a beautiful mare with large liquid brown eyes:

"Your Grace is uniquely your own. Some aspects of your personal Grace remain unknown to you at this time. Now is the moment to explore and discover the depths within you . . .

"Grace, you are now asked to help others, both in the realm of horses and the human realm, to discover their own hidden talents and truly recognize them as their Grace."

Grace answers the Pronouncement:

*"I will continue to do all that I can to shine a light on
each individual's special natural gifts, so that they may
recognize them and give thanks"*
Eponalisa, *The Fall Ride,* Melisa Pearce 2009

The moment I set eyes on her, I felt an energetic shock wave
heart connection, from just a tiny photo posted on Facebook
in early July 2012. Something about this exquisite mare called
to me. I sighed deeply and felt her magic. Melisa Pearce had
posted the photo announcing the arrival at her barn of a
beautiful Gypsy Vanner mare appropriately named Rhiannon.
What a delightful creature for Melisa's birthday gift! Of
course, I immediately began to hear in my head portions of
the 1970's song "Rhiannon" sung by Stevie Nicks of Fleetwood
Mac.

Long ago, in Ireland and the United Kingdom, Gypsy
Vanners pulled the cloth-canopied caravans of Irish Travellers,
also known as Gypsies. The wagon was the family's home. It
was where they slept and where they kept their belongings,
their tarot decks and other magical paraphernalia, and the
wares they peddled. Irish Travellers were known for their
skills in healing and their keen insight in trading horses.
While some scoffed at their nomadic ways, others honored
their folk wisdom.

Smaller versions of draft horses, Gypsy Vanners come in
a variety of colors and have abundant, flowing, thick manes
and tails.

There are many versions of the Celtic myth in which
Rhiannon is a gracious, bountiful queen-goddess. Rhiannon
is often depicted with horses or riding a white horse. She is

closely associated with the goddess Epona, which means "Great Mare." Epona is a protector of horses, mules, and donkeys. She and her horses are said to lead the soul into the afterlife.

In the Touched by a Horse certification program, I've found a community that honors my unique gifts and my unique spiritual journey. I first learned of the program in early December 2011 when I attended a program in which Melisa was a featured speaker. My husband and a dear friend accompanied me to the event because I was in a weakened state after experiencing a traumatic family event. As I listened to Melisa that night, I felt the restrictive bands around my heart begin to loosen. I wasn't sure what it was about Melisa that resonated with me, but she was able to put into words what I had experienced with horses—including the fact that they could be very healing. I enrolled in the program.

I had previously experienced the clearing of energy by a horse, but I had no idea how to describe what had happened. I was visiting my ten-year-old gray Quarter Horse mare, Firefly, my beloved companion and saddle horse whom I had raised since she was a yearling. I boarded her on the twenty-acre pasture that was not an environment conducive to spiritual experience. Other boarders included urban cowboys who strutted about in $350 beaver skin cowboy hats and chaps laden with conchos. They interacted little with their horses and spent their time gossiping and swapping tales. They were also great at giving me unsolicited advice.

On a particularly energy sapping, grief filled day, Firefly approached me. She was not even haltered. She gently nudged me with her nose and backed me up against my husband's white SUV. She placed her nose on the area of my chest above my heart. She nibbled and nibbled, breathed deeply, and worked her lips. Over and over, she yawned. It sort of tickled.

I wondered what she was doing. She hadn't done this before. My body began to relax. My heart slowed. I could feel a sort of humming vibration in my body. Firefly worked on me for about ten minutes. With a few more large yawns, she pressed her nose to my chest and fell asleep. I didn't want to move, but I was beginning to feel embarrassed because the urban cowboys were staring at us. I closed my eyes and rested into her. I felt calm and peaceful, and I didn't want it to end. I wanted to stay out there in the warm fall sun, surrounded by this mare's precious love. I felt better, released.

When the contact ended, one of the urban cowboys mumbled, "Guess that mare just wanted to spend some quality time with her mom."

From the looks on their faces, I could tell they did not know what to make of what they had just witnessed. I think we all walked away with a new awareness. For once they had no advice to give me. My husband placed his arm around me in support. He was touched, too. My smiles came easily later that day, even after I returned to reality and routines.

At my third CORE training session in the certification program, I was delighted to see Rhiannon waiting in the round pen as we entered Melisa's barn. Rhiannon has presence. She is a solid large-boned beauty with mahogany patches on her white coat, as if kissed by the Goddess herself. Angel-like feathers adorn her firmly grounded large feet. Her thick forelock cascades downward, covering her soft eyes. She has a distinctive dark mark on her muzzle that gives her a look of whimsy. She is a mature, Mother Earth type horse. It was as if a spell had come over me and I was drawn to her once again.

That morning, when Melisa invited students to engage, I quickly volunteered to participate in a "reflective" piece. My heart overruled my usually cautious behavior. I leapt from my seat because I couldn't resist working with Rhiannon. Melisa had placed an array of items on the table next to her to assist with guidance in doing personal work and connecting with Spirit. Included were Melisa's *Whispers from a Horse's Heart* cards, tarot cards, polished stones with words inscribed on them, angel cards, and various other items. Students could select whatever attracted them.

Sitting in a chair across from Melisa, I decided to pick something from a small mesh bag with a tie string. It contained brightly hued stones cut into slices and tiny balls slightly bigger than marbles, which seemed an odd combination. I thought the stones were probably scratching the balls. The balls reminded me of tiny translucent metallic gray-blue-green garden gazing balls. I was clueless about their significance and doubted that whatever was in the bag would provide guidance.

Ah, but Rhiannon! I wanted to get close to the magnificent and magical Rhiannon!

I fumbled around in the little cloth bag. My fingers found a ball in the corner of the bag and I drew it out. I opened my hand to reveal it, and it twinkled like a miniature of the star-filled universe.

Melisa said, "Those balls have been in that bag for seven years together, and I have never seen one that looks like that. Not sure what they have been doing in there all this time!"

Yeah, right, I thought. I doubted that my being there or touching it had anything to do with changing the appearance of the ball.

"Who do you work with?" Melisa asked. "What do you call them? Angels? Guides?" She explained that she works with angels.

"Uh, guides," I said. I didn't think myself worthy of attention from the angels. I had been aware of one angel in my life, but I wouldn't reveal that. I was afraid to show what was locked within—the spiritual side of me, a part I didn't understand.

Melisa told me to ground myself. She instructed me to place my feet squarely on the earth and breathe. She said my guides would give me a word. "Universe" or "universal" immediately popped into my head. But there was something more. Trans . . . trans . . . transcendence? Seriously?

Melisa and I simultaneously said, "Transcendence." That was the word my guides gave to me? I was dumbfounded. What did it mean?

Melisa sent me into the round pen with Rhiannon. Puzzled, I stopped to ground and open myself. My heart already sought Rhiannon, and I was joyous to be in her presence. I walked to the center of the round pen. Rhiannon followed and joined me. She reached out with her neck and gently put her nose to my chest for a moment. She loosened the grief buried within as my nose filled with her sweet horsey smell. I felt her all around me and within me. Our two energies mingled. She walked past my right side, stopping briefly. She then passed quite close, bumping me in the back. Her large feet barely missed stepping on mine as she aligned herself on my left side. Her head and lips brushed over the top of my head. Then she faced forward, close to my side, her heart chakra in line with mine, and she went to work, breathing and licking, opening and closing her mouth, drawing out and clearing energy from my battered heart and being. I felt my subtle vibration level start to lighten.

Melisa's seemingly disembodied voice came to me from outside the round pen. My focus was on Rhiannon. Melisa asked me to send my energy into the ground and then draw it up and imagine that I was looking down on my city, state, country, and the earth. Within seconds, I was part of the great universe, with its twinkling stars. I felt multitudes of energetic beings around me and we were all connected by love. I felt joy. I felt beings I had previously known in the earthly realm—some of them horse friends and other animal friends. I was fascinated.

Melisa quickly called me back. Rhiannon was right there with me, still working, pulling off layers of grief. Melisa sent my energy out a second time. The experience was even stronger—so strong that my knees weakened and I grew dizzy, as if I were being separated from my physical body. I wanted to stay in this transcendent state. I wanted to go home, where all energy is one, connected in love and joy in the vastness of the universe. I wanted to know more, feel more. I was tired of being separated, tired of the struggle in the physical world.

Melisa called me back and grounded me again. Rhiannon went to my right side and finished the task of balancing my energy. Melisa sent me to transcend the physical and be reunited with the spiritual for a third time. I already knew it was not yet my time to stay there. On the second trip, I had been so fascinated with what was happening that I nearly forgot all earthly attachments. I had been amazed at how quickly one can transcend the physical and reach the spiritual realm. With something like telepathy, the energetic beings conveyed that I was to return to the earthly realm, but that I now had a very quick access door to the Ascended Master Healers and to divine healing energy.

I later came to understand this energy as the positive motivating energy force of the universe—creative, restorative, and healing energy—and the Ascended Master Healers as the spiritual entities who carry this divine energy from its universal source.

When I returned from my third transcendent experience, I leaned against Rhiannon to thank her for her amazing work. My heart was cleared of grief. I felt lighter. The love, joy, and connection I felt in that transcendent place remained with me. I lay my head on Rhiannon's wide shoulder. Tears of relief and release ran down my cheeks and spilled onto Rhiannon. As I prepared to leave the round pen, I looked between the strands of Rhiannon's forelock and found one of her eyes. In it was the image of the twinkling stars that I'd seen in the little gazing ball.

What had I just experienced? I was awestruck. My legs wobbled as I left the round pen. My vision was blurred the rest of the day. It took days—and more—to process it. Of course, I've questioned it too. Had I been hypnotized? Perhaps it was sleep deprivation. I'd spent the night before that class watching the hours tick by, fearing that I might not make the 7:00 a.m. start.

I've come to understand that Rhiannon and other horses naturally clear and balance chakras. They check each other's energetic vibrations to sense whether all is well or something is amiss and needs adjusting. As prey animals, they depend for their survival on sensitivity to their environments. They don't have the higher processing parts of the brain that humans have. When they sense something amiss in the environment, they don't stand around second-guessing or examining possibilities. The herd moves in unison to get out of harm's way.

Humans and horses have these same seven major energy centers located in the body. Clearing blocked energy from emotions, or the body, frees up awareness in the mind. Body, emotions, and mind are all interconnected. Sometimes blocked energy needs to be cleared so all these areas can reconnect. The experience of universal transcendence created a new and deeper sense of interconnectedness for me. Somehow, I've integrated the experience. Even my thoughts cannot override the changes I experienced in my body, emotions, heart, and spirit.

With gestalt techniques, the foundation of the TBAH program, one need not tell one's story, nor even speak of the unspeakable. The objective is to get blocked or stuck energy and emotion flowing through a creative experience that leads to awareness, insight, and clarity. I am doing my personal healing in this program, and like other students, I seek personal growth as I complete the requirements for certification.

Many years ago, I had a strong connection to Spirit, the term I use for the divine energy of the universe. As circumstances and life challenges continued to stack up against me, trauma, pain, grief, fear, anger, and self-doubt resulted in feelings of abandonment. For more than a decade, I felt cut off and separated. I was afraid to have a full range of emotions, unable to feel any sustainable joy in life. I was mentally, emotionally, and physically exhausted and I buried the spirituality I once had in a deep dark closet within my heart. I hid my inner light.

Eventually, the humbling of my own heart has led to deep compassion and love for others. This kindled my desire to reach out to others like me and support them for a time as they traverse the pathway that leads away from fear, grief, and loss towards healing. It seemed the natural course of action. I am profoundly grateful and willing to be of service.

Yes, I have wandered through the valley of deep shadow referred to in the scriptures. Like many humans, I have given in to fear. I am returning to the path of love and I am reconnecting to what felt lost. Though I feel a calling, my spiritual journey is not the evangelist's journey. The TBAH certification program includes a learning tool about temperament types, which helps to explain this spiritual dimension. I am a high INFJ; I(introvert) N(intuitive), F(feeling), J(judging) type. INFJ's often feel a spiritual calling. It is not unusual, abnormal, or paranormal for INFJ's to have spiritual experiences.

TBAH offers the opportunity for each student to discover his or her unique healing powers—and learn how to exercise them. We all have gifts; our talents differ. Horses also have unique gifts and abilities that they demonstrate in differing ways.

Since my experience with Rhiannon, I've accepted the healing power of my heart and my hands. I can now extend it to others. Several sensitive students seem to recognize the change in me. One student asked if it would be okay if she felt my heart. I told her yes, and she placed her hand on my chest. After a few moments she gazed at me with light in her eyes and a beaming smile. "Wow!" she said. A couple of other students have also recognized that I am a healer, and they say that they can feel the warmth in my hands or in the energy around me, drawing them in.

Horses also recognize healers. TBAH coach Peggy MacArthur tells of the occasion, five years ago, when a horse she met spent time licking, leeching, drawing, and clearing energy from her hands. The horse recognized her healing hands.

While I have long known that I could be moved by the divine healing energy of the universe, I feared it. I dared not present my hands to horses. I wasn't sure I wanted that sort of validation. I now realize that even before my experience with Rhiannon, horses knew and responded to my gift. Several approached me and touched their noses to my chest in recognition. My six-year-old mustang, Great Spirit, often greets me by touching his nose to my heart.

Recently, a friend and fellow TBAH student did an equine gestalt coaching session with Spirit and me. When I entered the round pen, Spirit immediately went to my left hand, which he licked over and over. Then he went to my right hand and licked, but not as much. Finally, he gave my hand a tiny nip. I understood what he meant: "Now you know. Get on with it!"

My wild Mustang boy knows grief and loss, having been torn from his mother and his herd before he was weaned. Spirit was gathered along with his pony-sized half-brother, Little Bear, from the same Wyoming band. Both foals were separated from their mothers by the helicopters chasing them. The Bureau of Land Management sent them to a Colorado foal rescue. They shared the same pen, but Little Bear died of colic a few months later in captivity. I adopted Spirit as a yearling, and he grew up to be a very big boy. He now supports me and partners with me in doing healing and energy work.

I've learned to trust the somatic signals that occur when I should pay attention to someone who comes into my energy field and may need support. My heart warms and my left hand warms and tingles when I am moved to do something. For now, I sit on those hands, not knowing exactly what to do. To learn and gain more understanding, I am taking Reiki training with TBAH coach and Reiki Master, Peggy MacArthur.

While many students in the TBAH certification program plan to build a coaching business in one form or another, I'm on a different journey. I plan to use the knowledge and skills I gain through the program to advance the mission and vision of a nonprofit organization Spirit Horse Alliance.

The organization isn't named for my beloved Mustang boy, although he's an eager and gifted participant in our programs. Spirit Horse Alliance focuses on the power of horses to heal the human soul. We create meaningful connections between people and horses. We help people deal with unfinished business—including personal, career, and family issues. Horses touch us, transform us, and teach us about life, love, and loss. The Equine Gestalt Coaching Method is now an integral part of our programs. I am partnering with TBAH students and graduates and others to offer programs that are small in scale and huge in impact. My focus is primarily working with other women who are trauma survivors. We are just beginning to offer services for veterans with Post-Traumatic Stress Injury (PTSI). Not only am I a trauma survivor, but my son returned from deployments in Afghanistan and Iraq with PTSI and is eighty percent disabled from his combat service in the Army.

My personal growth continues. I still have difficult days. I'm still processing grief from years of pushing through it and stuffing it back down. Sometimes I acknowledge to the horses that my heart hurts, although it is not nearly as intense as it once was. On those days, I bring to memory my life-altering experience with Melisa, a remarkable teacher and healer Rhiannon, a magical horse, and a small twinkling gazing ball. I focus on the words given to me by my guides: "Universal Transcendence." In a split second, I can feel the love, joy, connection, and healing energy of the universe. I give thanks.

Paula Karen, MLS, is a horsewoman, writer and community leader. Among her greatest joys is participating in the magic that occurs when people and horses connect. She has extensive professional experience inspiring people to achieve personal and spiritual growth and healing. Paula is founding president of Spirit Horse Alliance, a Colorado nonprofit organization. Hawkflight Coaching is her newly formed coaching business. She is also guardian and partner of two amazing horses she has raised and trained since they were yearlings. Horses have long called to Paula. It is her honor and passion to love and care for them—young, injured, aging, wild ones, and all those in between.

Paula Karen
www.spirithorsealliance.com
www.Hawkflight.com

Manifesting Serenity

Samantha Marshall

Sometimes experiences are predictable and sometimes they change your life's direction in the blink of an eye. I have had a few of these pivotal moments, but never so monumentally as my experience with a horse named Fancy.

My life partner David (aka Dr. Mac) got an invitation to come to Colorado and do a talk on nutrition, his specialty and field of expertise. He traveled quite often to do these talks and he always asked me if I wanted to go. Until this Colorado trip I had always said no since I am not big on the chore of traveling. However, when he asked this time, much to our surprise, we both heard me say yes—and without a moment's hesitation or thought on my part. I stood there, blinked, took a breath, and thought, *Wow, that was quite different.*

He looked at me and asked, "Are you sure?"

I said, "I guess so. I don't think that was my decision." Still a little puzzled, but feeling it was right, I made my plans to go.

While at the meeting, I met Melisa Pearce, a person new to me but whom Dr. Mac had already met. I felt that immediate connection I sometimes experience with someone I meet and feel I've met before. As the evening ended, Melisa invited us to her house for dinner the following evening. David told me she owned horses. I was happy to be with a horseperson and very interested to get to know her better. We were delighted and accepted quickly.

During the dinner conversation Melisa explained that she combined gestalt therapy and horses in her practice. I was fascinated beyond belief. She could tell that and asked if I would like to experience it.

"Yes, yes, a resounding yes," I replied.

We set a time to arrive at her facility the next morning.

Horses have always had a huge place in my heart, so I was very excited the next morning as we again drove up to Melisa's beautiful ranch. As a child, I was at the barn where I grew up in Portland, Maine, as much as I was allowed. I had the joy of working with many different horses: Morgans, Pacers, Tennessee Walkers, and the Maine state champion five-gaited horse, Windswept Golden Dawn. The barn I went to also gave riding lessons and supplied horses to a summer camp a little further upstate, so we had some plain old good horses, too.

Unfortunately, my family moved to Arizona when I was a teenager, so I had to make the switch to Quarter horses. I had horses for my children and owned and operated a boarding and training facility in Scottsdale, Arizona, which was also the home field for the polo team. Later, my oldest son had a stable of ten for cutting and team penning, which I had the pleasure of riding. Yet, other than these times, the pressures of family and business kept my equine friends on the periphery of my life for many years. I was overjoyed to be back in a barn amidst the sounds and smells of my favorite creatures and happy to get the chance to get close to them again.

Melisa, David, and I walked the stalls and visited with each horse as Melisa introduced us and gave us a little background on them before heading for the arena and the famous round pen. There we were to meet a 1600-pound Gypsy Vanner draft horse named Fancy.

Fancy had just arrived from the Deep South, where she'd been miserable in the heat and humidity. She had immediately benefited from the clear, thin, cool air of Colorado. She was huge and beautiful with her black-and-white markings and big furry feet. She had never done this kind of work before, but it didn't matter because she was a natural. She was also a powerful energy worker and powerful healer. She had an absolutely masterful intuitive grasp of it, right from the outset. She had been watching from her stall since her arrival and had observed what the other horses were doing. My guess is that she thought, *Oh, so that's what we're doing here.*

Melisa asked me how afraid I was to go into the round pen with her, on a scale of zero to ten, with ten being very afraid and zero being unafraid.

I said, "It never entered my mind, so I guess not at all."

"Good," she said. "When you're ready, I would like you to go into the center of the round pen."

Bear in mind that Fancy did not have a halter on, or a lead rope, or anything. She was completely free to move about the round pen as she pleased, and she had met me for the first time only this minute, so we were strangers to one another.

David and two of our friends were standing at the rail outside the round pen and Fancy had strolled over to visit with them for a bit. Fancy was quite interested in David and was nibbling on the backs of his hands. She was probably saying to him, "You like to talk a lot."

That's true, by the way.

Melisa told them to step back from the rail. Then she told me to go to the center of the round pen and when I did, to close my eyes, center and ground myself, and go to a favorite place where I felt peaceful in my mind. "Nod your head when you're done," she said. "Now, imagine a horse, any horse, any breed, any size or color walking up to you from your left side."

This was where Fancy was in relation to me.

"Ground yourself in the spirit of horse," she added.

The moment I did that, Fancy turned and started to move. Even with my eyes closed, I could hear and feel this massive creature coming toward me.

Melisa warned, "She has really big feet, so be careful."

So, still keeping my eyes closed, I quickly put my feet together. I could hear and smell her as she came gently alongside me on the left. And then, amazingly, she leaned into me. She was warm and strong, and I felt a huge rush of energy pour into me. Wow! I had never felt anything so powerful before. She stayed there for a few minutes and then she walked around me to my right side. Again, she leaned into me and I felt another surge of loving energy fill my heart and body. I was told by those observing that she literally lifted her outside feet off the ground when she leaned into me and gave me her love and her healing energy. It felt like she was downloading universal love. She did the same on both sides.

When I opened my eyes and hugged her, the emotion I felt was overpowering and brought me to tears. My feet did not touch the ground for the rest of the day, and all I could think about was Fancy. I was so filled with love, it was magical.

And something else happened. The full spirit of equus came powering back into my life and reawakened my passion. I told David, "I have to do this. I have to learn how to share this with others. I need to do this program now."

I had no idea how it was going to happen because the company David worked for was having difficulties. Carving out the financing just didn't look possible because the budget was prioritized for many other things. But in my heart I knew this was to be my life's mission: my two greatest loves joined together—personal empowerment and horses. So I kept positive thoughts and knew it would happen, somehow. I knew it was right and had to be.

Sadly, but in right order, my dad passed on and left me enough to pay for the program, the travel expenses, and everything else I would need to do the certification program. I am continually grateful to him for his contribution to making it possible.

Within three months I was starting my new life, the one I was born to do. Fancy, who started it all, was stricken by a virus toward the end of my training and taken from us long before her time, but not before she had helped and healed so many. All I have to do is remember her and my heart opens up again and is filled with love—hers and mine. She'll never be gone for me as long as I am alive, and I intend to keep her memory alive by sharing her story with others.

Now I am a fully certified Equine Gestalt Coach with EGCM, living in northern Vermont. I have a spectacularly beautiful property and coaching facility. And guess what? It was another horse that showed me the way—this time a horse named Shadow. What happened was one of those "against all odds" stories that life is all about. Everything came together and fell into place perfectly, and I felt so blessed.

I was in Colorado at a training, and it was at a point in my life when everything was up in the air. Changes were inevitable, but I had no idea what they would end up looking like in the end. We were living in New Hampshire, and the company that both David and I had been working with was going down fast. We were figuring out what our next move was to be. As far as I was concerned, we needed to go back to California, so I could not only begin my EGCM equine gestalt practice, but also be close to my grandkids and family. I was absolutely certain that was to be our direction because I figured that the high income, high density, next big thing mentality of ritzy Orange County would be a perfect place to set up my business. I'd seen some awesome horse properties in San Juan Capistrano and I visited with someone who wanted to sell sixteen acres there. But the house was a shack and the price was $15,000,000.

Meanwhile, David was offered a *perfect* position in Vermont, doing exactly what he is meant to do.

"Vermont?" I said. "Are you kidding? That's the opposite direction from California."

My frustration was at an all-time high. What was I to do? So, I was back in Colorado at one of my final trainings and Melisa was showing us how we could do quick pieces of work by using her wonderful *Touched by a Horse Inspirational Cards* deck. I volunteered to do a piece. We sat as usual, took a deep breath, and centered. She handed me the deck, and without any instruction or thought about anything, she asked me to shuffle and pick a card. I chose "Direction." This was not a surprise.

Melisa asked how the card applied in my life right then. I laughed and said, "It's right on because I'm trying to figure out if I should go to California, find a place for us, and start my business there now. David would have a nice long commute! On the other hand, should I tag along with him to Vermont?"

David's new boss had told him he could move anywhere he wanted as soon as he got to know all the people he would be working with and was familiar with the system. That might take six months to a year. I had always planned for my business to be in California. Despite growing up in Maine, I had lived in California long enough to feel like I was from there. Besides, my family was there and I had connections there. Plus, I loved the weather. I could practice all year long and definitely thought that was where my market was.

Melisa asked that Shadow, a sweet, wise gelding, be brought to the round pen. He had been doing this work for quite a while and definitely knew what he was doing. Melisa sent me into the round pen and asked me to divide it in half. Next, I was to walk across the center from one side to the other, turn to the right, and start walking around the inside edge of the round pen. I was instructed to talk about choosing to go to California, speaking out loud about what it would be like, how I would feel, what I would do, what my life would look like, and anything else important.

So off I went. Shadow just stood there looking at me. When I reached my starting point, Melisa instructed me to cross the round pen again. But this time, when I reached the other side, I was to turn to the left and start talking about moving to Vermont—what would that be like, what were my feelings about it were, and why might I do that. No sooner was the first sentence out of my mouth than Shadow partnered up with me and walked beside me around that half of the round pen.

I repeated the process, only this time I reversed it. That is, I turned to the left and started walking while talking about California. Shadow stopped and watched. Then I turned to the left and started walking while talking about Vermont. Again, Shadow partnered with me as I walked and talked about Vermont. That said it all. He clearly was telling me to go to Vermont with David. I was puzzled and not so happy, since I really wanted to go to California, but I took the coaching and went to Vermont. I was still resistant at first, thinking that I wouldn't stay for long.

We moved into a nice enough house with five acres, and at first I thought I might be able to have a couple of horses and start my work. But it was an awkward piece of land with a steep-walled creek that would have been dangerous and a huge flat lawn that would have turned to mud.

"Fine," I said. "Time to find a barn nearby."

We found a psychologist a few miles away who had an empty barn and was intrigued by what I was proposing, but was nervous about liability. There was another nice facility with an arena, but everything was a long way off, so we had to rule that one out too. I needed to be close to my horses. And anyway, since I planned to do four-day retreats, where would everybody stay?

And then it happened. David rarely got sick, but something got the better of him one day, and when his boss requested a meeting, David suggested they "walk and talk" to minimize the risk of him sharing the virus. They took off up the unassuming dirt road next to our place, and when David came back, he was practically jumping up and down with excitement. About a mile up, they had crested a ridge and there it was: a spectacular property with a barn and other outbuildings. And the barn was empty! What's more, it had a "For Sale" sign at the end of the driveway.

We knew we couldn't possibly afford the seven-figure tag. Not yet, anyway. The property was way out of our price range, but I had learned to dream, think, visualize, and manifest. Maybe, just maybe, some kind of a miracle might happen.

On a whim, I turned up the long driveway to the place one summer day not long after discovering it. I wanted to just get a sense of what it would feel like to live there. That's part of the manifestation process, as you may know. I figured the place was empty, since I had seen no signs of people. As I cruised the driveway circle in front of the house, I was startled to see an older woman sitting on the porch. I soon discovered that she was the family grandma.

"Are you interested in the house?" she asked.

"Oh, it's absolutely beautiful. I wish I could buy it," I replied.

"Well come in and take a look," she said, getting up from her chair. "Just leave your car there."

Inside, it was even more beautiful than I had expected, with floors and cabinets of natural cherry and a stunning master suite with an office with views that stretched for miles. There were several guest bedrooms and an attached guest-house with its own gorgeous kitchen and another three bedrooms. Clearly, there was lots of room for clients to stay and sweeping views across what would be the paddocks and barn. It was simply, unimaginably perfect.

Off to the barn we went.

"It's pretty new," she said, "with three stalls and space for two more."

I was so excited. I thought that I could at least rent the barn and get started. After all, it was just sitting there. But then everything began to happen.

I started to see myself in the house and horses in the barn. I was imagining how I would set everything up and what it would feel like to be living there. I told David and he said, "Well, it's absolutely perfect and I know we're going to be there, but I have no idea how we're going to pull it off."

No matter. I told my friends—the positive, supportive ones—all about it and how perfect it was. A few weeks later one of them came to visit and I said, "Let's go up and I'll show you the barn."

My friend said, "Okay. This is your place. I will visualize you here every time I think of you."

I sent a picture from the listing to a couple of other friends and asked them to see me living there.

I drove up again and asked the family grandpa if he thought it would be possible to lease the barn. He said I would have to talk to Bob, the owner. A few days later I was painting the porch on our house and a couple pulled in and strode up. They were the owners of our dream home.

"We hear you're interested in our property," the man said. "We have a feeling from what Grandma and Grandpa have said that you may be the right people to have it. I'm going to make you an offer you can't refuse."

As it happens, they had built a house in town, twenty-five miles away, to be closer to their kids' schools. They needed to get their country home sold. Not only did it have a barn and twenty-five acres of pasture, but it also had another 120+ acres of forest for riding trails. And although it would still be a stretch, the price he proposed was now tantalizingly within reach!

That left only one problem. We had a long-term lease with a purchase option on our existing home. We would have to get out of that lease in order to move on a short timeline. The landlord was visibly crestfallen when we said we were no longer going to buy, so the only way out was to sell the house for him. How would we do that in a down market? Intent, that's how. Pure intent. We sold the house for him in three days, above asking price, and moved within a month. How did we manage to move in so quickly? Well, David has the world's best boss. He gave David his performance bonus six months early so we could make the deposit. He wanted us to have the place, too.

As I write this, I'm looking out of the office windows I talked about earlier. We are planning the arena, the turnouts, and the extra stalls. I am getting ready to schedule joint ventures, cores, and retreats. And I've already been featured in the local paper. David is thrilled, and if it's daylight and he's not at work, he's outside being a country boy. Although our activity level is far from serene, we have named our place Serenity. It just goes to show that the impossible can happen if you believe it you can make it so.

Thanks, Shadow! I never would have been living my dream without you. And my heartfelt thanks to Melisa for creating the EGCM certification program so I could fulfill my mission in life. Plus, I pass on big thanks to all the others who help me along the way.

These are two examples of how God/angels/the universe provides and puts all the pieces in place when it is meant to be. All I had to do is to say, "Yes and yes, I'm ready to do this work. I'm committed to helping horses fulfill their mission here and now, which is to help and heal humans."

I kept moving forward in faith and it happened. Now I'm on to the next step in manifesting and completing my mission.

Samantha Marshall is the author of Understanding Children through Astrology which is in its 3rd edition and available through all major sources. In addition to doing regular astrology chart readings, she is also doing readings on horses to uncover their needs and abilities plus compatibility with their human counterparts. She is a Certified Equine Gestalt Coach from the internationally recognized Touched by a Horse Equine Gestalt Coaching Method. She is combining astrology, horses, gestalt therapy, and coaching to help others clear blocks, develop leadership skills, establish self-empowerment and/or self-esteem. She loves assisting people to get free from limiting beliefs that may be holding them back in any way from living an authentic joyful life.

Samantha lives in Vermont on her beautiful property, Serenity Ranch, with her healing herd. She is coaching and hosting retreats on a variety of topics.

Samantha Marshall
Certified Equine Gestalt Coach
www.equiserene.com
www.equineastrology.com

An Opening Within

Trena Anderson

I want to share with you one of my most profound experiences, both as a woman with over thirty years of horse experience and as an Equine Gestalt Coach. These are two very different perspectives and the difference between them lies in the fact that humans who own horses have a very basic knowledge and understanding of what the horses' needs are while the Equine Gestalt Coach has come to understand and connect with the spiritual knowledge equus offers—an entirely new process of connection and healing. That horses can play a part in mankind's healing is growing in human awareness, and Melisa Pearce's Touched by a Horse Equine Gestalt Coaching Method has opened a door to greater understanding of this.

Horses have clairsentient abilities within them that we as humans are only just beginning to tap into and become conscious of. Horses are also able to read a person's energetic field, and when we educate ourselves about what the horse's response means, they can communicate and partner with us. When we allow ourselves to simply follow the energy of the moment and pay close attention to what the horse brings to our awareness, there is a profound shifting of energy and awareness that can result in the healing of physical and emotional traumas.

The story that follows is one such experience. I share this with the utmost respect to both my client as well as my equine partner. We humans have much to learn about the impact of horses and their ability to heal, as well as the bravery of clients who step forward and allow a healing herd and coach to be a part of their personal journey.

The day began with an afternoon client scheduled for a 1:00 p.m. appointment. I knew that this particular young woman had a background with horses, but beyond that basic knowledge I knew little about her. I was not concerned with any details of her history, nor did I have any prior knowledge of what was "coming up for her," that is, whether she was experiencing physical or emotional challenges. Having recently graduated, I was learning to trust the process, trust what I had learned in the program, trust myself, and most of all, trust all my spiritual partners in my healing herd. All of this comes from a very simple, yet imperative, new way of being. With trust and presence, the area that needs attention will easily arise to the surface to be looked at for resolution.

As I headed out to catch a horse for my session, I was quite surprised when my main gelding, Sundance, stepped up immediately asking to "work." As a horsewoman, I have come to realize that when heading out to catch a horse for a ride or excursion, the horse I have chosen is not always excited to go to work and does not meet me at the fence in anticipation. No doubt, many other horse people have also had this experience. However, since becoming a graduate of this program I can honestly admit that my healing herd has already discussed who is the most appropriate partner for a client prior to a client's arrival and the candidate is eagerly at the gate awaiting their turn to provide loving assistance, support, and knowledge.

In my herd, Sundance, a Buckskin Appaloosa, is the main man. He is very forthright and quite solid in stature (15hh). At times he can be very bossy, but he can also be a comedian. Sundance often steps forward when the client is struggling with self-confidence and boundaries. He is also the chakra balancer in the herd. He has no shortage of self-esteem and truly thinks he is a comic. However, at times he does have a tendency to carry these antics to the extreme.

For instance, when Kim Beer, a professional photographer, came out to take pictures for our website, she mentioned out loud that it would be very cool to take some action pictures. Sundance immediately took off running, tail high in the air, and every time he passed Kim, he bucked and reared like that of a wild mustang. This was funny in the moment, and Kim got the shots she needed in the first five minutes. But my laughter was wearing thin when twenty minutes later, as I was attempting to catch him, he was still carousing around the pen like a wild man—with the whole herd now involved. And that is

Sundance. He is always the show-off and yet he is one of my main partners in this line of work because he never ceases to amaze me with his knowledge and awareness.

Sundance is also my daughter's horse. She has worked with him in our local 4-H program for over seven years. Over time, I have seen that he can be a very gentle soul when he chooses. When he first came to us through a friend, I was wary of putting an inexperienced nine-year-old girl on a four-year-old horse. This combination brought up so many questions about safety, trust, and inexperience. Yet Jordyne rode him for six hours straight that first day when we went to "try him out" and not once was there a falter on his behalf. Even then, he was doing his work of showing us to simply trust in the process.

When Sundance offered himself up that day, I confirmed that we were preparing to go to work. For those unfamiliar with the Equine Gestalt process, this "work" is exactly as the process name describes it: gestalt work with horses. Gestalt work involves an inward exploration of self. Partnered with the horse's healing abilities, it allows the client to gain insights and awareness to the parts of self that have become disconnected. Through this gestalt experience, the client is able to reconnect these disconnected parts and return them to a "whole," returning energy flow and movement to progress forward in a healthy direction. This natural integration opens the door for the client to recognize that they have the answers within them. As coaches, we and our equine partners simply ask questions that open up the space for this to happen. We perceive the areas where energy is blocked or stuck and assist in reestablishing the flow of energy. Rather than reacting from the fragmented parts of themself that hold charges, the client experiences a reconnection of all parts of self that shifts their space and being, both within and beyond reestablishing the flow of energy and movement, and they begin operating from a "whole" sense of being.

On that particular day, when Sundance and I were clear that we would be working together, I haltered him and brought him into the round pen area to wait for the arrival of our client.

When she arrived I settled in and became aware of the young woman's energy field. Physically, in my body, I became aware of a particular area that felt restricted in terms of the energy flow. This is a form of somatics. I began to move forward. I asked her a question relating to the sensation I was experiencing and she acknowledged that she was aware of that feeling within. I asked about the intensity of this feeling and at what age she first realized it was a part of her being. She more fully described her impression of that feeling and what she thought it related to. At this point, she was unable to recognize when it first came into being. As her coach, I sensed that this was where the energy was impacted. I was aware that she had disconnected herself from her body, so I moved forward gently with a few more questions to bring awareness to the area we were focusing on. My awareness arose from within, as together with my partner, Sundance, I recognized that we could assist her in opening up that flow and moving into a more open place of consciousness with a very simple tool.

As she moved into the round pen, I immediately noticed that although she was an experienced horsewoman, Sundance walked away from her and simply chose to observe her from a distance. This confirmed what I had sensed earlier I was reminded that she had stepped out of her heart/body and was operating from her head. Horses connect with people who are connected to themselves. They have no interest in showing up for someone who is not being in the present moment or being in their body, and they will almost always disengage. Sundance's response communicated to me that she was busy thinking instead of being in the moment.

This is a very common experience in the beginning for most of my clients. And, unfortunately, it is where most of us as humans have come from for a long time—our heads rather than our hearts. It is also one of the most precious things our horses can teach us: to be present and to connect to ourselves and our bodies.

I asked my client to begin walking forward and to sense the earth beneath her feet as she moved. Together, we moved through a brief breathing exercise that calmly allowed her to become more aware of and be more in touch with her physical body. We began a breath cycle at her crown chakra (the top of her head), traveled down through the rest of her body, and moved out through the bottom of her feet. I asked her to imagine growing roots deep into the earth's center.

Immediately I saw a shift in Sundance as his ears pricked forward and he became engaged. He observed her and then began to move forward into her energy bubble. As he approached her, I could sense that she was slightly surprised. She continued forward on her path with him glued to her side.

I chuckle within as I recall the moment in my own experience when I doubted the horse's awareness and I chuckle every time as this natural progression of breathing is acknowledged and I observe how quickly the horse reconnects. Once again I am amazed and feel very blessed to have had this tool shared with me and to be able to connect within myself and honour the awareness of the situation. This experience was no exception. I was amused, amazed, and humbled.

I asked my client to move into the center of the round pen and allow Sundance to move around her as he chose. As she stood, he began at the bottom of her feet sniffing gently and slightly pawing at the sand around her feet. She stiffened a bit and he immediately lifted his nose as if to say, "No worries. You are safe." As she relaxed, he went back to his job of sensing and then clearing the energy in her field. He traveled up her front side, spending some extra time in her stomach and chest area. At times he almost bit at the chords of energy, yet never once did more than place his lips on her. As he reached the top of her head, he moved around to the backside of her body.

As Sundance was doing his work, I asked the client to explain what she was experiencing. She was at a loss for words and could only utter, "Indescribable," and "Filling up with a new sense of lightness." Together we relaxed into the moment and Sundance soon let me know he had now completed this area.

Next I had my client move forward to envelop this new sense of being. I asked her several questions and followed the energy within her responses to guide us into the next step of our work. She shared with me a construct around "not being allowed" and brought up a recent conversation in which she felt guilt and shame—her automatic reaction versus what she would have considered a healthy response. She recognized that she had reacted with a trigger and did not understand what had caused this reaction. I asked her more questions and noted that she was moving forward once again, but now in a different direction.

I observed Sundance's response to her statements. There were times when he remained in step at her side. Yet, as she talked, there were moments when he refused to move forward. This immediately let me know that although my client was "sharing freely," there were parts within her that were incongruent. This can sometimes be looked upon as the story parts of ourselves or projections, which are parts we have taken on and made our own that are actually from others' points of views. And while we may not realize that they are really not a part of us, our spirit from within knows different. The horse's connection to her heart and soul easily showed to me that there was another area within in which we did not have true energy flow. I blessed my partner's response and acknowledged his awareness, and we began to move into another process to unravel the energy around that problem.

I brought what I call my polarity pole into our round pen and repeated aloud the words my client had shared. She narrowed down the two aspects within herself that she struggled with most. We picked a distance on each side of the pole that represented for her the meaning of each and how she saw herself in each of the sides. For her, the aspects at battle were the "realistic" and the "possibility" sides of herself. Together, we began to look at and embrace each of these parts that had served her at different times in her life.

At one particular point, Sundance actually picked up the pole and dropped it in her lap, signifying his acknowledgment of her awareness. Through his action, I had the opportunity to see how she lit up when she opened to and resonated with the flow of energy that represented what was right for her. And I was able to witness her perspective broadening. Sundance helped her experience that she was fully capable of moving closer into the lightness her spirit yearned while still embracing those parts within that had been important and useful to her. It no longer needed to be either-or. And this was important because being able to embrace her differing qualities would strengthen her as a whole person.

This experiential process related to the Access Consciousness® training I'd had. That model views everyone as infinite beings who are everything. It is recognition that we are "all." And with that sense of being all, there is no judgment. That opens the space for us to give up the need to be defined. We can easily accept this new "being" of allowing ourselves to be whatever is necessary in the moment, and new possibilities begin to open. For my client, this simple process moved her into an even bigger expansion of awareness.

As we completed the polarity pole experiment, I immediately became aware of a much larger area of energy coming to the surface to be looked at. As an empath and intuitive, I am able to sense the energetic field and the vibratory frequencies of most people, and I was very drawn to this particular line of work because it resonates with the awareness within me. Having the opportunity to shift my own awareness through the experiential path of my own spiritual journey with gestalt and Access has allowed me to become conscious of and embrace all the different parts of myself. This newfound self-acceptance has given me the chance to reconnect on a more universal level to a much higher consciousness and has opened for me more possibilities on many levels from which I can choose. In this moment, we moved into one of the greatest experiences I have been blessed to have in this work.

I observed my client from the outside of the round pen. An abundance of energy began to rise amidst the calmness of her physical being. Tears rose to the surface of her dark lashes and began to fall gently, absorbed into the dark sand. Sundance immediately came up alongside her, lining up his heart chakra beside hers. He literally wrapped his head and neck around her body in an attempt to embrace her entire being.

At first, she relaxed into his simple presence, but then she shifted. And once again I sensed a separation within her between what she allowed herself from this physical connection and what she could have through it. I opened the space to her awareness with some gentle questions and I observed awareness return to her physical body. I simply asked Sundance if he could show to us what energy, space, and consciousness each of us could connect to that would open up the infinite possibilities available.

I watched Sundance as he moved in front of her and then gently dropped down on his knees before her until he was simply lying flat out in front of her. I was amazed and in awe at his choice of action. This gelding is always on alert within our herd. I have never witnessed him even lying in the sun, let alone drop his guard and lie before her in an ultimate display of vulnerability.

She was stunned at first. She couldn't believe that he was actually lying before her with his head gently in the sand. She asked if he was okay. I explained that I had never before witnessed this behavior from him, but that I trusted him and what he was doing. I asked her what the display meant to her.

The first words that came out of her mouth were "trust" and "the ability to be vulnerable." I asked where in her life she did not allow herself to be these aspects, and in that moment, she began to sob. She shared that as a teenager, she'd had a young filly with whom she truly connected. They grew up together. Sundance's behavior was an example of the safety and vulnerability she and her mare had shared. As she began to provide memories of her childhood, I invited her to join Sundance on the ground and allow herself to open up to those lost feelings of security and trust. She knelt and leaned against his neck, sobbing and releasing all the years of pent up hurt and anguish, and she shared that she had cut herself off from the ability to embody those aspects.

This new space opened up to an incident in her childhood in which she had been trusting and innocent and an adult had betrayed her trust. All the hurt and pain around that moment in her life came flooding forward and outward. In his honouring of her spirit, Sundance simply lifted his head as if to encompass her body and envelop her in his sacred safe space. Within moments she grew quiet. I could sense a huge shift in the arena—quietness and lightness had entered as she let go of the enormous burden she had carried.

She lifted her head from Sundance's shoulder and rose from the sand. Her body moved freely and appeared almost weightless. As she stood up onto the solid ground beneath her feet, Sundance rose and joined her at her side. The connection they now shared in this moment simply was an honoring of one another. She thanked him and reached out to give his neck a huge hug. He solidly accepted what she offered as thanks for his assistance, and then he slowly made his way round to the pen door, as if to say, "Thank you for allowing me to be a part of your healing process my lady, and I will gladly follow you out the door with the utmost of respect, if you'll reach me that pail of oats on your way out."

Trena Anderson is the worldwide coordinator and founder of Connecting In Spirit. She has completed training in Access Consciousness Foundation, Level One, and is a certified Bars practitioner. She has certification as a Reiki Master and Equine Gestalt Coach. Her talents of connecting with her gifts of intuitive awareness and empathic abilities, as well as her education in several other energy modalities, has allowed her to partner easily with the healing powers and presence that equus has to offer. With over thirty years' experience in the horse industry as owner, trainer, breeder and almost a decade of experience as a 4-H leader, Trena has the horsemanship knowledge and the vibrational awareness to connect with both the horse's innate energetic abilities as well as those of the client—even for those who have never been in contact with horses.

Connecting with the horse's freedom of spirit, presence in Being, and the magic of their sentient nature combined with her own clarity of spiritual senses allows her to connect to her client's vibrational field. This holistic approach opens new doors to awareness and elicits immediate shifts and lasting change on the client's behalf. She shares this healing gift of Connecting in Spirit with others whom are ready to reestablish their own connections within themselves and the world around them.

Trena Anderson
www.ConnectingInSpirit.com

When Tomorrow Comes

Caroll Ellis and Gilbert Nell

It is the way of things, comings and goings.
We are a breed apart you and I,
and I receiving the better part of it for sure.
Forever altered this view I have
of what is love and my place in its time.
Our first encounter, I the smarter one I thought, but now?
After this time of ours?

For human I am and human I will always be.
Judgments now passed, place an equality on the both of us
and better off the result am I. Eyes opened no
longer blind to what is life and value found.

We are a breed apart yet new arrivals every day increase our
herd, from history's path worn down from abuse and neglect.

Though paths diverge and different horizons see,
there is a new dawn arising better for the both of us
and like-minded souls a kindred make.

Childhood does end and in its place a nobler breed
of life evolves.

Carroll Ellis is the daughter of Gilbert Nell. They have collaborated on many things over the years, including taking the same electronics class in college and serving in the military. Carroll's new career path is with the Touched by a Horse certification program. At her facility, Ellisian Fields Farm Ltd., she helps veterans and people of all ages move beyond traumatically stressful events.

Carroll Ellis
Your habits become your character.
ellisianfieldsfarm@gmail.com
www.ellisianfieldsfarm.com

About the Editor

Melisa Pearce is the founder of Touched by a Horse® and creator of the Equine Gestalt Coaching Method®. As a result of many requests to share her knowledge and method, the Equine Gestalt Coaching Method (EGCM) Certification Program began in 2008. Today she has students and graduates throughout North America.

Melisa is author of the Amazon best-selling inspiration deck, *Whispers from a Horse's Heart*, in collaboration with artist Jan Taylor. She is also author of the award winning book, *Eponalisa*, a contributor to the book *Horse as Teacher*, and coauthor of *Games People Play with Horses*. Additionally, Melisa has several audio recordings of guided imagery that tackle topics like manifesting the future, balancing the chakras, and creating abundance.

Melisa lives in Niwot, Colorado with her husband, Dane Cheek, her herd of equine partners, and a veritable menagerie of animals.

You can find more information about Melisa Pearce, her groundbreaking work, and her certification program at:

http://www.touchedbyahorse.com
http://www.egcmethod.com
http://www.equispiritual.com
http://www.eponalisa.com
303-440-7125
Toll Free: 866-652-8704

Like her on Facebook:
http://www.facebook.com/touchedbyahorse

Follow her on Twitter:
http://www.twitter.com/TouchedbyaHorse

Are you ready to be "Touched by a Horse®?"